PSYCHIC CHANGE

PSYCHIC CHANGE

THE SPIRITUAL SHIFT FROM VICTIMHOOD TO RESPONSIBILITY

amielle zay marcotte

House of Marcotte

Published by House of Marcotte, Mercer Island
https://houseofmarcotte.com/

Cover design: Rachel Marek
Cover image credit: © Rudchenko Liliia/Shutterstock

ISBN (paperback): 978-1-7376848-3-1
ISBN (e-book): 978-1-7376848-1-7

First edition

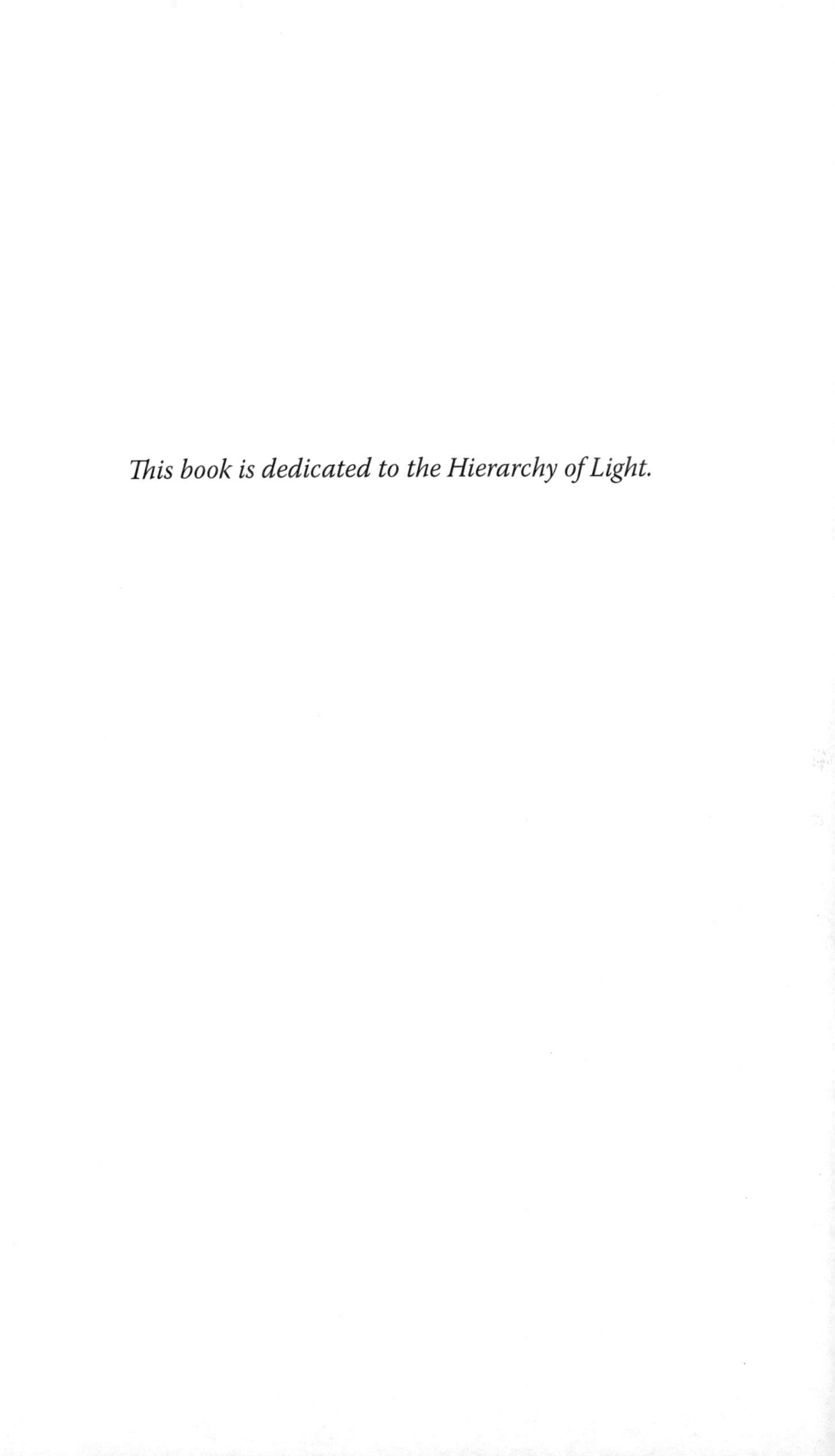

This book is dedicated to the Hierarchy of Light.

CONTENTS

PREFACE ix

INTRODUCTION xv

PART I 1

CHAPTER 1: *The Spiritual Principle of Truthfulness* 3

CHAPTER 2: *The Spiritual Principle of Individualism* 17

CHAPTER 3: *The Spiritual Principle of Love* 36

PART II 61

CHAPTER 4: *Out of the Fog* 63

CHAPTER 5: *The Spiritual Principle of I Am* 92

INTERLUDE: *The Secret Knowledge of Miracles in Session* . . . 99

CHAPTER 6: *The Spiritual Principle of Oneness* 114

EPILOGUE 131

ACKNOWLEDGMENTS .133

ABOUT THE AUTHOR 135

PREFACE

This book is not intended to create controversy, nor is it affiliated with any religious group. It is also not written to promote any dogma. I am not a formally trained theologian, nor do I purport to be an expert in any specific religion, monotheistic or otherwise. I am respectful of a multitude of faiths.

This book has been written based on my deeply held spiritual experiences. It is a direct result of seeking sustainable higher consciousness as a way of spiritually ascending while on the Earth plane. Its main purpose has manifested as an honest attempt to serve my Divine life purpose of world service. My mission is to support individuals in understanding their Godliness by illuminating the Power of integral strength within them. I do this by empowering others to see they are the path and the destination they seek to awakening to the great mystery of life. By taking responsibility for the consciousness we carry through a commitment to sobriety and the path of enlightenment, we become the peaceful solution. One in light is majority. I continue to work with sacred texts and teachers in the spiritual realm, and I also hold sacred space for those I am gifted to work with by Divine appointment.

This entire book is dedicated to inspiring the reader to become familiar with the spiritual principles in place within our Earth plane, as well as how the directional nature of these principles come alive when we acknowledge them through the medium of light. We are the medium, and light energy is what we have the potential to harness within us. Our light is mystified gold dust, an unexplainable sustenance we get to experience as it connects to us through spiritual principles. The acknowledgment of this connection produces both alignment and ascension in consciousness.

It is my humble attempt in rightly relating my life to these spiritual principles by identifying real-world scenarios that showcased my lack of understanding of *it all*. I reveal where I bought into the lie that I was separate from my source of good, thereby falling into the abyss of victimhood. Victimhood is a state of orphanhood. It's where I sat spiritually; therefore, it's where I stood emotionally. In this suffering state of isolation, going to my inner light was not possible because I was rejecting my connection to the One Who Has All Power and All Knowledge.

In this self-rejected state, my only option was to go outside of myself to meet my basic needs. The action of going outside of myself to meet my essential needs, like love, activated the ego in its negative form. Through the negative ego, I identified the things *I did* as my identity. The ego believes that *what we do* is who we are. So if anything disrupts this sense of identity (the thing that I am doing), my whole world collapses around me.

This collapse further perpetuates the victimhood state, and negative emotions seem justified. Hence, foundations of fear are not sustainable because they require the action of going outside of ourselves to meet our needs. Going outside of ourselves to meet our needs is the very opposite of taking responsibility for our life and becoming self-reliant. However, from this victimhood state, the only foundation of life available to me was a foundation of fear—but fear is *the lie*.

I built my world to cover up *the lie* and was susceptible to *lack* as a result. Lying and lacking are the antidotes of truth and prosperity. I alone was responsible for rejecting myself and negating the flow of truth and prosperity. By buying into the lie as a way of life, the fear of separateness and feelings of unworthiness were my default. No matter what I changed on the outside, it wasn't enough. It was as though I was rearranging deck chairs on the *Titanic*.

It was only through a steady seeking of higher consciousness, while following precise ways of being, that I had a gigantic jump in consciousness—then another, then another, and so on. Invisible light stuff began entering my consciousness, highlighting a life beyond my wildest dreams. Recognizing the invisible light inside of me also drew my awareness to the invisible light stuff inside of others. I saw that the light had great potential. All of a sudden, my psyche shifted, and even newer principles became available to my consciousness. Principles that were just words the day before became complete entities and spheres of sacred movement—and they were everywhere. A bundle of grace flowed into my life, and grace moved from being a word into a spiritual experience I now carried.

The power of spiritual principle appropriation was at hand. The erroneous core belief of separateness dissolved, and all behaviors associated with the lie of fear also vanished. Then— the psychic change happened for me. I became truly grateful for who I am, what I have, and what I am doing here. I was the same person, on the same planet, but *how* I was experiencing letters, words, numbers, and equations was altogether unique. I took my next breath effortlessly: *ahhh*, miracles were in session! Stoked on these principles of light, I began aligning with them in every single situation, joyously having faith in their power.

The truth had come through the light. I came to acknowledge the *spiritual nature* of light. I acquired a deep reverence for what I could barely explain. The principles were words, but they were also the governing rules of a larger puzzle. The vision to see them wasn't there one second, and then in the next, the words made sense and carried profound depth. This was all very exciting. I wondered, if this clarity had actually been here all along, then *what else* was here, ready to be discovered?

The principles carried light, and their essence was connected to the greater light that I and everyone else was carrying. We—humanity—were all interconnected. *Wow.* I immediately began to cultivate an intimate relationship with the light principles. Light and Spirit were synonymous. Light and Spirit were infinite. I noticed that in my application of a spiritual principle, everyone became attracted to the action behind it. The principle magnetically attracted similar energy, magnifying its potential. This synthesized intention and power within my newly integrated humanoid system. Being the carrier of this light brought forth great humility. The insanity of going outside of myself to meet all of my needs had ended. It all came from within now.

Spiritual principles have a multiplying outcome; they exponentiate. In applying spiritual principles, we raise our consciousness and have access to greater portions of creation. Atonement is being one with our light. It's connecting to our light and allowing our light to connect with spiritual principles. Becoming aligned with these spiritual principles activates our unique gifts and talents within a service protocol. One in light is majority. We allow our perpetual rise in consciousness through light. In seeking higher consciousness, we get to uncover knowledge within us that is already in place. Within is where we get to know the One (where all power and all knowledge live).

My personal stories capture the essence of spiritual principles in action. By seeking higher consciousness, I became aware of them through my evolutionary, transformational psychic change. The psychic change I experienced continues to be an unfolding process. Spiritual principles serve as keys to locked light codes, here and eternally, in unimaginable ways.

Specifically, they open invisible doors. Using these keys has become a privilege of this life, a privilege generated from an inner-freedom consciousness. This inner-freedom consciousness generated an ideal life for me in return, with circumstances that complement my natural gifts and talents. All of this has been obtained by solely relying on the application of spiritual principles as a way of life, rooted deeply in my mission to serve the good of all.

INTRODUCTION

Every person has that one moment in life when something big happens, and from then on, your life is defined by two parts: before the event and after. Clarity strikes like lightning from the sky, and revelations dissolve more of the veils in consciousness. For some awaken through performance principles, while others cultivate awareness through cause-and-effect cycles. Our individual seeking of a greater understanding of ourselves and our universe propels us forward into a devoted submission to the work and purpose assigned to us at birth. To not seek in the kingdom of eternity is to become susceptible to the suffering of idleness, which, in turn, propels personal resistance to the inevitable nature of change. All tangible results, then, are a manifestation of our conscious alignment with the responsibility of pursuing our life's work.

Within the 144th light ray from the sun (where Earth is), there are a select few who resonate extremely bright spectrums of light. By mere presence alone, a rise in consciousness is transmitted upon interacting with these beings. They are gatekeepers of invisible doors only made visible by one's determination to go all the way inside. These masters of light are antennas for higher frequencies and can translate numbers and sounds from a universal code into our earthly order. By design, masters of light are a force to be reckoned with.

Competitive action is the training tool for achieving awareness of separation. As we progress through the various levels of life, we "believe" the idea that winning brings forth success. From the eyes of a child, we become aware that we are separate from others through race, creed, and culture. If we are athletic, then size, sex, and speed further categorize us. If we are intellectual, then how fast, how much, and how young we acquire knowledge propels us. Our test scores become leveraged for advancement. Like energy attracts like energy. The race is on as kids start competing over everything. We are compared and contrasted with our siblings and our neighbors. We are taught the symbolism of flags and colors, which draws deeper lines in the sand. As children, we literally look up to our parents (the big people) as giants, relying upon them to care for us. Depending on how aware our giants are, family dynamics become the nucleus in one of two ways.

Firstly, our families can be in full alignment and participation with spiritual principles, which is wonderful. Or secondly, our families are out of alignment, and we learn this through their actions. Either way, conditioned behavior dominates the organization of our cell growth and how we build our worlds. The latter imprint (being out of alignment with spiritual principles) through our experiences, demonstrates we were raised by wolves and the animalistic survival game begins for us. In time, if we choose to awaken to this animalistic imprint, we become aware of all sorts of distortions like parents competing for our love. We, in turn, compete with our siblings for our parents' love, and through it all we learn to associate favoritism with love. Out of this, we experience one of the darkest forms of separation, known as jealousy. This negative emotion and all of its countless friends are the by-products of a foundation established in fear. There is nothing scarier than having to be a favorite of someone to receive love or be in someone's good favor to receive love. Both of these create the belief that love is outside of us and its possibility unattainable. In this misalignment, we can try really hard to please others and even succeed, but the "success" is short-lived and will, sadly, never be enough.

From there, we remain in an unsatisfiable state. Success is defined by how well we perform and, specifically, how well we can organize our inner structures (mind, body, and spirit) without any real idea of how our humanoid system works. The amount of wasted time spent on these outward activities is endless, and the amount of energy they consume is relentless. If, however, our "giants" are not operating under the illusion of separateness—we can then adopt their consciousness of connection and reap the benefits of applying spiritual principles tenfold.

Our whole world is a reflection of a sustainable ecosystem that continues to build upon itself as we activate the gifts and talents given to us at birth. It is as though God personally waters our gardens on a daily basis, ensuring the lush abundance of our spiritual journey. We are one with Mother Earth; our journey becomes an astounding adventure as we continue performing our earthly duties in the Great Work. The Great Work is defined in building a harmonic world. We are citizens of the miracle of life, and life is grace. Everything works out for us as it should. Each application of a spiritual principle aligns us further with all of creation, and our usefulness continues to multiply, like nature, by numbers.

Life is a level playing field. Develop whatever story you desire about the before and after, but spend minimal time in these places, because life is action, and action is right now in the present tense. It's a great idea to gain a healthy perspective about life before birth and after death, however, in order to have the best possible experience while living. The absolute best portions of creation await us in our honest attempt to come to know the principles of light. In the activation of our light, we get to become aware of the soul structure, a structure we carry within our humanoid system that is our zero point of nothingness. Nothingness is everything-ness. This is important to know.

Another word for principle is "law," and the laws that govern our existence are irreversible and unchangeable. Search them, know them. Together, let's get with the master program. Our uniqueness, when rightly aligned, creates right thinking and subsequent right action—thus, our consciousness is lifted. We progress into a greater understanding of who we are and what we are doing in this space-time continuum (the physical universe). We operate from our ideas of who we are and what is possible. In order to have a greater understanding, spiritual principle alignment is essential, and it opens us up to portals where vision and imagination flow.

We all experience life in different cycles. These cycles are characterized by the tests we must fulfill through light. Through light, we get to progress and ascend into a joyous exploration of creation. The map legend, or key to our "map for life," is filled with the navigational guidance known as our emotions. Our emotional bodies live in full light on the astral plane and become known to us as our light bodies manifest. Knowledge like this is revealed as "ahhhh" revelations as we become aligned with as little as one spiritual principle at a time. Awareness of our emotional state combined with an eagerness to align humbly with spiritual principles opens a door to an enchanting experience. Emotional well-being is a state in which we actively participate in and seek understanding of how to transmute our lower natures into useful and magnetic forces. It is when we gain full vision of who and what we are, as well as what we are doing here, that we embody the spiritual principles fully.

The psychic change came about in my life through seeking higher consciousness. I had no idea what exactly I was looking for, but my seeking continued to lead me down a path of illumination where my perception of life encountered a drastic shift. It was as though I had walked through an invisible door that I didn't even know was there. In going deeper within myself, I unknowingly was going deeper into spiritual principles. This is because spiritual principles are light principles; one magnifies the other. They are filled with light, and they also connect with the light we all carry. When working with the principles, I visualize light, because that's what automatically comes to mind—and giving my attention to the "light stuff" brings forth beautiful life. Prior to having awareness of the light, my emotions were unidentified flying objects. Yes, UFOs!

Having no placement or context for my emotions made me feel inadequate. I was unable to transmute my emotions into a higher order. I was defeated by insufficient actions: actions that resulted from being separated from my inner portal of light. I fell into a cycle of running from my emotions, fighting them, and doing whatever it took to hide from them. My coping mechanisms quickly turned into huge liabilities, preventing me from having a fully activated life.

This book speaks to the importance of taking responsibility for who we are. It is my hope to support you in relating to the behaviors and reactions that come due to a lack of inner-portal access through my own real-world scenarios. I will talk deeply about personal accounts and how the application of spiritual principles unfolded in my life, particularly through the unimaginable healing that occurred with the application of faith and forgiveness. This freeing process let loose a lifetime of victimization, a deception that was the direct result of growing up with my human will centered on the egoic self. Being unaware of how to integrate the human will with the will of God (an assimilation of soul, spirit, and mind), the world's appearance continued to be confusing and hazardous.

An entire chapter is devoted to the mysterious *love* principle, and how when this principle is completely aligned with all other spiritual principles—they are all experienced simultaneously. We then arrive in the land of humility, where access to this love level is only revealed by the precise arrangement of the superconsciousness and the subconsciousness—and, of course, the main qualifying gem: a sincere heart. The promise of this book is that there will be a shift in how you come to know things through acceptance and diligent practice. This I know for certain!

The final expression of this book offers insightful knowledge about our inner portals to greater consciousness. This is the mighty space where energy lives and extends far beyond our understanding—yet we can directly impact it through transmutation of the lower-natured self, resulting in a purification process. After purification takes place, transformation arrives with the keys to access greater portions of creation. In raising our consciousness by consistently accessing our inner portals (as well as applying spiritual principles), we are transported into a superstate. We can even enter a "gap," or space, of infinite expansion and intelligence.

I inadvertently entered this space twice and was rocketed into a dimension that was indescribable. In this infinite superstate gap, greater portions of creation become available to us. I became so mesmerized by all of this that abandoning myself to this mysterious greater consciousness became effortless. It brought so much joy to my life and to the lives of those around me. Through this joy, I discovered my Divine life purpose was to help others come to know spiritual principles as a way of life. I am wholeheartedly grateful for having your attention on this matter!

My ever-increasing well-being has set me on a steadfast and immovable path of continuing to take responsibility for my consciousness. I will reveal methods I used in my soul-searching process during the miraculous discovery of the phenomenal superstate gap, and how this gap opened a treasure chest filled with new keys for the doors I am currently seeking. I believe I've been called to write this book, and that through its writing, I will inevitably cultivate new doors that will be revealed to me in time. So, just know that you have my full undivided attention in these matters, because my spiritual success is contingent upon the success of yours. Let us now commence upon our journey through the beautiful process of psychic change!

PART I

CHAPTER 1

THE SPIRITUAL PRINCIPLE OF TRUTHFULNESS

*Strength: From the survival of the fittest
to admitting personal powerlessness.*

Angelic, she sat before me.

Two pristine white Watermill sofas faced each other, both well preserved. On one side, the consciousness of what a yoga path could afford, and on the other side, the inner freedom of what the twelve steps of recovery could afford. In the one o'clock position hung a rustic wooden cross over several shades of white stucco. Behind this enchanting woman stood a horizontal column of forest-green Italian cypress trees. The verticality of these entities demanded a deep reverence as they defined the horizon and the limitation of human. Their growth patterns spiraled upward with a force that not only defied gravity but also left their limbs no choice but to follow suit and grow into the tree's center. There was a bougainvillea garden to my left. It wasn't fully visible from where I sat, but its vivid purple-fuchsia color was reflected onto the balcony. The opened French doors made connecting to the garden possible.

I looked down at my sweat-stained yoga clothes. I felt like I was not enough. With all the fervor of a cheerleader rooting for the losing team, I said, "These are warrior clothes!" The last thing I wanted was to appear unsuited or ungrateful in front of her and God. It was all I had to offer at this point, an appearance of what I presented to the world. I heard an old tape stream through my consciousness: *Looking the part is 90 percent.*

I had relied heavily on that technique, but dressing up had stopped working. It was a fun part of the equation, but it certainly did not assist me in feeling comfortable in my own skin. Feeling comfortable in my skin was a process of purification. Part of the process of this purification meant refraining from going outside of myself to feel whole. This meant letting go of my fancy wardrobe since I often hid beneath it. This also meant surrendering "the need" to purchase things altogether. I often fell into the thought pattern of *Everything would be perfect if only I had that one dress.* That one dress could solve the great equation of peace per my mind's direction—a direction I was learning to humbly yield to, with the understanding that I am not my thoughts.

In response to the volume and sole proprietorship of my thinking, a simple *Is that true?* question would arrest my mind's intensity to do dumb things fast. The "is that true" (ITT) technique allowed space for acknowledging the thought without accepting it as law. Within our internal governments and our humanoid systems, action is predicated by agreements made within our minds. These agreements form beliefs. Beliefs are woven intricately to build a structure. We live within the confines of these structures. With the ITT technique, we address all of the faulty beliefs generated from erroneous core beliefs, and we go straight to the core belief responsible for a polluted system.

With an honest appraisal of my thoughts, feelings, behaviors, and constant self-assessment of unworthiness—it was time to give personal powerlessness a sincere attempt. Could personal powerlessness give access to truthfulness? Why did I have a burning desire to be truthful? After all, I hadn't told lies to people, had I? Accepting that there was something happening in my inner-child work that I didn't know about yet, I continued.

The other part of what was happening in the purification process was accepting that I *am* already everything. When I fully accept my wholeness, then all of my actions become powerful because I *am* full. From a full state, what is needed in the moment arrives to support my life contract. Our life contract activates as a direct result of letting go of the belief of separateness. The gifts and talents already within us become available to us. In alignment, we gain access to truthfulness. This is not something we can do alone. This is where admission of personal powerlessness translates to getting out of our own way in order to be that which we are. How can you understand something you don't even know exists? You can't. That which you are is the *I am*.

Feeling incredibly vulnerable, it was a great deal of effort to peer into her eyes. Embarrassment and shame came with my inner-child work. If we don't evolve emotionally due to childhood traumas, then we are at the emotional age of our inner child as adults. When that part of me is triggered, childlike behavior is my response, because that's where I sit emotionally. Being unaware of this, my coping mechanisms are my external solutions. Becoming aware of this pain and my ability to overcome it means that my solutions are internal. Exposure of the inner child can feel raw. Even with the best of all elements supporting my process, being able to listen is muted at times because of my fear of intimacy. Intimacy translates as "in-to-me-see." I was learning to be open to truthfulness because of a core belief of connectedness.

The core belief of connectedness is that I *am* connected to the One Who Has All Power and All Knowledge, and therefore I *am* connected to all things. Not mainstream truthfulness like "I didn't tell a lie today" (although that matters too), but a truthfulness that keeps delivering solutions to me for the good of all in every situation. Having access to truthfulness opens a gateway where more and more truthfulness is revealed to me right when I need it. The amount of conviction in my heart led me to believe the presence of something greater was here in this sacred space as I embraced my inner child with her and God. The presence of conviction is such a beautiful thing. I found the freedom of tears as they flowed out of me. Similar to the natural flow of a waterfall, tears cleanse and purify by catching flight on air molecules as mist. The mist then disperses the impurities further into nothingness. Already feeling the emotional lifting by the power of presence, my imagination was returning to me. I was self-assured that my personal powerlessness was my offering.

My asking for the presence of God brought forth a revelation: *We get to be truthful.* It's like my barriers became permeable where Spirit's essence could pass through. I commanded myself to meet her eyes. I connected with them. The connection with her eyes allowed for the promise of two merged in the name of the One Who Has All Power and All Knowledge to take place. Higher consciousness was fun. Feeling blessed, I made an agreement with myself: *I trust her.* Why? I'm not entirely sure, but she is who God presented as a teacher, and I am ready to learn. In a spiritual experience, it's really that simple. I had come to believe that God reveals itself through infinite channels, channels that I become increasingly grateful are open as a direct result of placing my reliance on the One Who Has All Power and All Knowledge.

She began to speak. "We are going to trace back the memories you have of abandonment until we reach the earliest recollection. I'd like you to recall the earliest memory of feeling alone. How old were you? Where were you? What was going on? What do you remember?"

There I stood, my inner child, some eight years old, at the door of the home I grew up in in the Deep South. The screen door was aluminum-like. Screen doors were a necessity here in a southern subtropical climate, the dominion of bloodsucking mosquitoes. Our ranch-style white brick home had a red shingled roof. The red and white on acres of green contrasted with our two magnificent oak trees with roots ten feet in diameter at the front of our property. This made for a gorgeous landscape. Our interior's flooring was 1970s green, complete with brown shag carpet and wood paneling on the walls. The pool/kitchen/bar area was on an open floor plan designed for hosting family and friend gatherings. Our C-Band satellite dish sat on the back of our property, and this was "the super-cool piece of technology" of its time. We were a big-fish family in a small pond. With my family's financial success, our home had all the bells and whistles that were to be envied. I would listen intently to Dad's detailed description of our home to others and then play hostess myself, giving walk-throughs to guests. He was proud of every element, even down to the diversity of limestone laid out over our long driveway and throughout our landscaping.

The home was situated in a country setting where rice and sugarcane fields separated properties from one other, and each neighbor was a car drive away. The highway we lived on was not busy. It was more of a country road, but as dusk settled, a greater number of cars would pass on that long, winding highway. What I knew is that the highway out front led to another highway named 10. When you got to the 10 highway, and made a left, the highway would take you all the way to California.

Like the sigh of a greased landing, I said, "California, yeah!" With sure-heartedness, I continued, "When I grow up, I'll be in California." Everyone knew it. Mainly because I told people every chance I had. I could hear my grandmother whispering in my mother's ear, "Where does she get these ideas from?" My mother never questioned my dreams or my imagination; instead, she encouraged them. She began dressing me up like a princess before I could walk and paraded me around in countless beauty contests. I began carrying a princess wand at the age of one, and I believed in its magic.

In my memory, the sun had already set, and I was inside the house behind the screen door. The car lights were beginning to pass along the highway. With the inner certainty of a high moral code born from pure innocence—I focused my eyes to see the farthest set of headlights coming down the highway. I wanted those headlights to be from my dad's vehicle, so I said, "Dad is coming!"

Growing up in the country was a blast. I rose each morning before the sun came up and reached into the greatest days of my life. The farmland made for a unique understanding of the seasons and the harvesting of vegetables and fruits. We recognized the smell of rain as nourishment. I made real mud pies after the blessings of rain, and then I would sell them to my cousins off the back of my big red three-wheeler. We made associations between weather and food—what food went with what weather. We would build forts in the woods where I ruled as a queen. I was always leading the march to the mark. Building things and doing things in a precise manner made my heart sing. I knew how to operate the machinery on our property, and I would (most of the time) persuade my cousins and friends to push their limits to learn new things.

Returning to her eyes, I recalled her original question—*my earliest memory of being alone?* Truthfulness entered. Of course, due to my overconfidence and persuasive ways, arrogance had now caught up to me, proving to be my worst enemy. This childish act would have at one time seemed comical, but now it was turning out to support the faulty core belief that *I am alone.* Because I'd awaited Dad's arrival so many times, I had come to believe I was alone, and then I learned how to be emotionally unavailable. The agreement within my mind was made, and my behaviors of overconfidence with the power of persuasion were the beginning of decades of overachieving and overcompensation. It was all right in front of me. The truth continued streaming through my consciousness. If anyone found out I didn't have a real dad, or a real family—I would die. The fear of death settled into my little eight-year-old princess dress, multiplying the momentum of tightly woven beliefs over and over and over that *I am alone* within the assembly line of my mind, moving at a manufactured rate.

Reflecting on the entire world of a "strong woman" I'd built, I began to have a new perspective. I began to see my world differently. "Strong" had always been applied from a place of struggle, the struggle of thinking I was alone. My response to a faulty core belief of being alone was to join the military, be a pilot, and pursue adrenaline sports that were dangerous. My mantra was "I am as strong as the things I am able to accomplish." Surrendering this identity in a state of personal powerlessness was not easy. These things identified me: they were my appearance, they were who I thought I was, and without them, who would I be? Yet here I sit in front of her and God entirely ready to have God remove the merciless obsession of *I am alone* and all the things attached to it.

Brain surgery: only God can do it. Pause. My head began pounding. I could hear my pulse through my ears. My pulse was countable in my head. The sweating of my palms commenced. The uncovering of what I already knew was the truth. I only had access to Truthfulness in my admission of personal powerlessness over what I saw as the root of my problem. Only I could see it, and only I had the ability to join the One Who Has All Power and All Knowledge. In order to get to the root, I began with my behavior. In this case, "overconfidence with persuasion and arrogance" was the behavior I need freedom from.

I knew that this behavior resulted from beliefs I had made agreements with in my mind. When I had the established core belief, *I am alone*, the foundation of my internal governing was a lie. Similar to when you tell a lie, then that lie requires another lie and so on—and until the truth could be revealed, I had built my whole world on the lie of being separated from God and therefore separated from my fellow loved ones. Every action I took was an attempt to try to cover the lie. We cannot operate from two different foundations; we are either connected or we are not. Thus, the music stops.

Pulling each other on a giant sled behind my big red three-wheeler brought us belly laughter. The sound of children playing brings everybody home for me. The day Dad arrived with my big red three-wheeler made waiting for him worthwhile. I wondered if he had personally walked to the North Pole and made the request to Santa himself. Gosh, the time in between grew both in length and devastation. More time behind the screen door was not enriching; instead, I was becoming more and more convinced that *I am alone.* When he did show up, he ensured I had the best of whatever was available.

Dad's persona was a lot, and he always made sure I knew he was better than me in whatever pursuit we engaged in. On summer days, we often raced each other in small sprints on the fresh-cut grass of our property. The smell of carbon-based molecules gave freshness to the air. It made me want to play. The laughter, the striving to go faster, the desire to earn Dad's favor by being his number one was always there. The joy of the family being together outside in nature was so lovely. Nightly family gatherings, which included my grandparents, were common. My father would praise the children where praise was due, complimenting things about us he observed as excellent. These were exhilarating moments, with grand applause in front of grandparents who doubled the glory.

Deep French dialect was spoken by my family. We always spoke very loudly and laughed even louder, as if everyone were outlaughing each other. The laughing was contagious and comical unto itself. The deep voice of my grandfather when he said the syllables of my name in perfect French dialect was heartwarming, as if he'd named me himself. His energy was a summoning of respect to the elders of the world. The respect of our elders was ingrained in us as children of southern tradition. This formality was packaged with other manners that were not questioned. Deeply rooted human conditioning had been passed along from generation to generation, and was very much looked down upon if challenged. Even if there was nothing respectable about the elder, you said nothing to challenge them. We were taught by action to sweep things under the rug, and keep things secret. I made the agreement: *what people thought mattered!*

A swampland was encompassed within our family property. It was a dark and haunting place where poisonous snakes and larger reptiles lived and roamed. God is there too, in nature's darker ecosystems, sustaining life as a primary purpose. As children, we looked at the skinny gravel road running parallel to our home and perpendicular to the highway out front as dark and creepy when it entered the swamp. We would only race through it on the big red three-wheeler, never stopping in fear of being eaten by a crocodile. I would full throttle the three-wheeler through it at top speeds.

The gravel road was about the width of the back tires. On both sides of the gravel were slimy green swamp waters, an alligator heaven. Moss and gray grass fungus hung from tree branches. Spiderwebs were draped everywhere. The croaking of frogs and a steady frequency of crickets were the ambient sound. The deeper into the swamp you got, the louder the ambient noise was—as if animals I hadn't met yet were sounding alerts of my infringement to larger animals. I loved making friends with birds, squirrels, rabbits, and any animal that would listen to me—but the swamp had things possessed with deadly bites, and there was a deep reverence for its unforgiving wild nature.

Our family was fortunate to have a beautiful in-ground swimming pool where swimming in safe waters was possible. I swam like a mermaid with the frogs in our pool as a daily adventure and caught dragonflies in my glass jar. Daily, by dusk, I was inside the house, bathed, and fighting to keep my eyes open from a hard day's play.

So there I stood, little Amielle some eight years old—another evening counting the headlights coming up the highway. I was really good at this. I knew what the headlights of each make and model looked like from standing at that front door, continuously waiting for Dad to come home. I don't know how many times I did this; all I know is that I would do it, and then I would come away from the door, giving up on Dad and our family unit. I can't remember the final time Dad came home. It's a bit of a blur.

Pain in my child's body prevailed. In pain, we experience disharmony. Disharmony is the absence of love. It is the breaking of a bond that is as unnatural as counterclockwise motion. Counterclockwise is the opposite of Divine flow. The entire world and all within it moves in a clockwise direction. The clockwise direction is the will of God. When we accept the truth of God's will, then we, too, open the pipeline to our Divine union. My father was my giant. He was the human I gave all my power to, and whom I looked up to for my sense of security. I was learning how to love by watching him. My identity became tangled in the false identity of his mistakes. His story became my story. He was me, and I was him. It was time to greet little Amielle from where she stood—behind that screen door, and I needed to welcome her home.

These events were happening so fast. My parents were going through a nasty divorce all of a sudden. It was tough to see and hear the hate. I was certain they were doing the best they could and that they would work it out. I needed to balance the vibrational lows within the family. I kept positive and happy no matter what. I was so positive that the family began to expect that demeanor from me. This was a lot of weight for a child to carry, trying to keep the family together. I made another agreement: *I am responsible for my family's emotional state.* The devastation of the dysfunctional family dynamic, and the remarriages of new people now added, got complicated. Confusion can only happen in the mind. Confusion is not a trait of the heart.

Being confused was a sign that I was almost solely relying on my mind. Now our fairy tale of a life, the very thing that was special about our family, was weighted by defeat. The worst thing to be was a big-fish family in a small pond. I endured embarrassing moments at school when teachers were nosy about my family's business. I've always wondered how adults aren't aware of how awake children are or how they innately know when someone really loves them. Children know a sacred safe space and when or if love is absent. I made an agreement: *I am strong.* This inner-child work I was up against in this moment was about freeing me and my soul so the cycle of survival could stop. After all, it was my agreements that I was here to address. Those survival agreements would no longer be necessary as a direct result of having the One Who Has All Power and All Knowledge lift my faulty core belief: *I am alone.*

It was uncomfortable to be here as my inner child, and I didn't see the value in returning to expose my family dynamics. I began to get angry. I was not feeling as trustworthy now as I had in the beginning of our sitting with one another. She, the trusted servant, was across from me, illuminating from within. I sat still, reliving the trauma of unaware and hurtful adults. When we are little, there is no separation. It's just big people and small people. I had this erroneous idea that big people, because of their height and authoritative control, were spiritually aware and good in general. Oftentimes, the clarity of my childhood consciousness proved this idea to be inaccurate. Because of the discrepancy between knowing right from wrong and experiencing *wrong* from the big people that surrounded me, I often felt responsible for taking care of myself and the adults around me. This childhood survival solution developed into an excruciating savior's complex as an adult. I developed powerful conditioning and character defects associated with feeling responsible for balancing the erratic emotional nature of those around me. Believe it or not, I even got high off this kind of power over adults when I was a child. In my mind, the authoritative character was a phony. The way adults lied to themselves and to each other and even to the children family dramas of family affected me as a developing young person. Over time, this saturated into a negative-ego consciousness outside of me, and I was swallowed whole.

In those childhood shoes, I unconsciously separated from the One, and I made my human will my sole power. In this way, I began to act out being alone by running the show of life as I saw fit. My perception from that point of separation was skewed, and I was at the center of my off-kilter perspective. I could never be disconnected from God, but my ego edged God out indefinitely. This is what I was experiencing for twenty-seven years, prior to the psychic change. My self-centeredness, of what I believed was best for me, was in choosing relationships based on the fear that I wasn't good enough (another form of lack). Relationships are where I played out the erroneous core beliefs I had self-developed, like *leave before you get left* or *leave without saying goodbye.* In the pre–psychic change, I was unaware. I had no other way. I was always looking for what I could get from any situation, placing myself inadvertently in a space of false freedom. A giving consciousness was not available to me, due to the negative core belief of unworthiness: *I am not enough.* I was in a life driven by ego, which was isolating—and a void was always present, the space I developed between my God consciousness and human will. I continued to try to fill that void with any- and everything, but it was an unbeatable black hole. Its consumption was endless, and no matter how great my intentions were, they were never enough.

When self does not get what it wants, it retaliates, which looks something like taking toys and leaving. The acting out of the ego, in this way, is childlike selfishness. The ego needs everyone to work for it, and when this doesn't happen, it has no other choice than to go elsewhere. After the psychic change, we seek a willingness to transform into a human of dignity and grace as our creator would have us be. We are comfortable with not knowing the all, because this is where God can truly be found. We actively seek our part and become assets to each mission we are assigned to, here in the miracle of life. The miracle is all-inclusive in togetherness, and we learn that *freedom* takes great responsibility in the accepting of who we are in this moment—and being willing to do something about it.

With courage, I continued the emotional exercise. I begrudgingly began to give thanks that she, the spirit guide across from me, was willing to do the inner-child work with me. In her full recognition of my faulty core belief and the knowing that, with God, it could be removed, she asked, "Are you ready to greet little Amielle?"

I nodded. "Yes."

"Okay, let's close our eyes," she said. "I'd like you to walk up to little Amielle and kneel down beside her. Ask to hold her hands, both of them, palm to palm. Introduce yourself. Tell her she no longer has to stand behind that screen door. Offer your love and protection to her. Have her understand that you are going to give her love and protection for eternity. State your promise of love for her. Now ask her to come with you. Lift her up. Embrace her fully. Now open the screen door and walk into the sunlight. Keep walking until it's so bright that you become one light."

With these words, I began to feel an overwhelming grace as this negative core belief (*I am alone*), which once ruled my world and left me defeated in my relations, began to lift. I felt lighter. I began to surrender to an outcome I hadn't even thought of yet.

It's amazing how our life events arrive at the most precise time for human evolution. Somewhere along the seeking of higher consciousness, it dawned on me that this inner-child work was necessary for me. This was and is something I must do in order to break the link in a chain of repeat, of history repeating itself. This was something profound and new for a humanity that desperately needs to heal inner hurting worlds. There was no hate or resentment toward my father or mother and their paths. They were only doing what they could to carry the torch amid the obstacles of their own conditioning. It was now time to go further and to carry the torch a little farther myself. It was time to add fuel to a torch that would light the path for those to enter my life next. Two words were evoked: "emotional well-being," words that sang like a canary. There was an inner freedom in my consciousness now. I had no idea what the future looked like, but I'd been liberated in ways I never could have imagined.

CHAPTER 2

THE SPIRITUAL PRINCIPLE OF INDIVIDUALISM

Spiritual sweat equity: YOGAIRFORCE is born.

It is said that when the soul aligns, all the forces of the universe come into play for our highest good. The soul is an entity that has a real existence; it is distinct and vastly independent. All the forces are spiritual principles, or laws of light that govern our existence. The universe suggests oneness in frequency. "Play" refers to the gifts and talents given to us at birth, which are meant to help us remember that we are children of the One Who Has All Power and All Knowledge. "For our" implies the soul living within us (us as humans). The soul living within all of us supports us, cheers us on, and knows the most direct route to our own individual life contract fulfillments. The "highest good" implies duality and choice. Within the universe, we have good and evil; good is in alignment with everything above, evil is out of alignment with the will of God—and choice is up to us.

My young adulthood arrived, and I discovered two things I fell in love with tenfold: *flying* and *yoga*. The minute I took the controls on that first flight—hidden talents, all strengths, and even perceived weaknesses were in full alignment and held accountable. My sense of purpose was heightened. It was like turning up the furnace within my soul. My first exposure to aviation was at my sweet-sixteenth birthday. I convinced my parents to gift me with my very first skydive. The first jump would be a tandem jump out of a Cessna aircraft, a janky little plane. Sitting on the floor of the seatless aircraft like two Siamese twins, the jumpmaster and I were fully geared from head to toe with D-Ring attachments, making us one unit. The pilot attempted the engine start several times prior to the prop accomplishing a full rotation. The pilot turned his head over his right shoulder and projected to us with a chuckle, "Cold start!"

He then put on his headset and reentered his zone of calibrated steam gauges that presented information in several different formats. He turned the instrument dials and pushed buttons in sequence. I watched him acutely as he began to speak into the headset. He was a little out of shape and took breaths from his mouth instead of his nose. This drew my attention to his belly, which was protruding over the seat belt.

I had developed a critical eye, a competitive eye with others. My attention to detail was survival based. It had become second nature to observe others, scanning for weaknesses and imperfections. This made me feel superior, and superior was safe. Feeling grandiose contributed to my arrogance of ignorance. This was the ignorance of believing I was alone in the world, which meant (a) I was responsible for all the good in my life, and (b) it was all up to me to make things happen. When our core belief is a lie based on illusions of separation from our source of good, then the foundation of our emotional being is not well. The only foundation available to us is fear. The spell and dark sorcery of *I am alone* is so devastating to our well-being, it has the power to derail our whole life or, even worse, make it so as true life never begins.

Because I operated from foundational fear, my negative ego resembled quicksand in its activation. This kept my life right below sea level. My actual default was in the negative. My ego identified with skydiving and made skydiving who I was. It was my identity; it was my personality. When others recognized my strength and bravery associated with skydiving, my ears perked right up. My ego loved the societal attributes associated with this daring sport. It would arouse them like heirlooms, making them totally mine. Having my peers find out that I was alone in the world scared me more than jumping from an airplane into midair. Being alone meant being unlovable. I was so embarrassed by the lie I suffered from; my ego wouldn't have it any other way, though, than to keep the lie buried. The courage I carried was rooted in attitudes of entitlement, since my skydiving centered around my ego. In my mind, I was responsible for all the good in my life. My train of thought was always *me*-based. Never once did it cross my mind that I could be an asset to life. The only thoughts available to me were the ones streaming from a negative ego: how I could be the best with all eyes on me.

The pilot's flow kept a steady pace as I steadily completed the tasks on the pilot's checklist all the way to takeoff. The pilot's flow added an unforgettable resonance. Due to sitting on the floor of the aircraft, my sight gauge was sky only until we were above four thousand feet up. Then we could remove our seat belts and prepare for the jump. With so many mechanical connections between the jumpmaster and me, minimal movement was essential for safety. I was processing the flight in live time. I hadn't even considered the flight prior to that day, only the skydiving. As a matter of fact, I had been studying skydiving for five years through magazines printed in California.

This was my first exposure to aviation. This would be my first free fall. There is no relativity to how high you are prior to the jump. It's not the same feeling as being on the top of a tall building and looking down. I had dreamed of body flights for many years. I was attracted to the relationship with the air and movement. I perceived this as a way of being free.

By the time my sixteenth birthday arrived, I had already primed my parents for the premeditated skydive. My parents knew I would find a way, and so they decided to grant my sweet-sixteen wish. There was a local skydiving school in our parish. I had given the skydiving school accreditation in light of their affiliation with national associations. I learned about it in the magazines. I regularly had skydiving publications delivered to our home. On the day of the jump, I attended safety ground school. It was a "marking" of the body-flight postures for the skydive.

The flight up was an interesting sight, with the jumpers and all of the gear piled on top of each other. We finally reached a jumpable height, and the adrenaline kicked in. It was pretty loud inside the airplane, like riding in the back of a truck. The jumper at the door gave a hand signal that he was going to open the door. Then he yelled, "Door!" The door opened, and the wind whipped into the aircraft and across our faces. The wind made it very real. I felt a thousand butterflies in my stomach. Within two to three seconds of sheer fear, followed by a tap on my shoulder, it was time to fly. We scooted our way toward the door. The jumpmaster yelled, "Ready?" In a body-rocking motion, he called, "One!" We swayed back and forth, and then he wailed, "Two!" Then, the final "Rock-a-by-fly, three!!!!" We launched into midair. Open space everywhere. Free. Light. Zero Gravity. Weightlessness was the reward that delivered ten seconds of indescribable freedom. *Ah!* It was everything I had ever dreamed. I'm a bird!

Eight years later, I sat in a much larger aircraft at the world-famous drop zone in Perris Valley, California. This aircraft allowed for a running start before launching into midair. With pro skydivers among us, I heard the magic words, "Door!" and it was time again. My childhood dream had taken flight. Sharing the cargo area of both a Twin Otter and Skyvan aircraft at fourteen thousand feet, with some of the most skilled skydivers in the world, expanded my horizons of what was possible. Everyone was so great. During this time, I loved the stories we shared, the laughs, and the high fives. It was brotherly to cross-check each other's gear on the ride up. Then, one by one, we exited into seconds of zero gravity with personalized style, reaching our individual terminal velocity of 120 miles per hour.

It didn't take long before a fellow jumper who'd just passed his pilot exam offered to take me flying in an R22 helicopter. *Wow.* On that flight, we launched from Long Beach, California, to Santa Catalina Island. We flew at fifty feet above the ocean with the doors of the helicopter removed. The pilot asked me if I would like to fly the helicopter. Without hesitation, I accepted his offer. Like clockwork, I used hand-eye coordination as best I could (check); spatial orientation (check); 3D orientation (check)! I knew right then that I was a pilot. The euphoria of my heart smiling on that flight was immeasurable. So unexpected yet so right. I thought my heart had risen into my cheeks and would stay there for all eternity. I was fascinated. From that point forward, I would fly with anyone who would take me flying. I would get checked out in every plane I could fly with my experience. I'd become an inspired aviator.

Aviation became everything to me. The people, the planes, the engines, the adventures, the fly-ins—all of it was true love. My quest to be an aviator had officially commenced. A couple I knew from the skydiving community offered to have me fly right seat in their 1957 Grumman Albatross seaplane for a period of time. This aircraft was being leased by the big energy drink company Red Bull. Since the aircraft didn't have an autopilot, I took on the position of keeping altitude while soaring around white puffy clouds. It was like a huge Tonka toy with wings. People loved it. We would carry Red Bull guests to and from some of the most sought-after aviation events, like Fleet Week. Fleet Week drew thousands of spectators. It was an opportunity for our Grumman Albatross seaplane to fly formation with America's Blue Angel jets.

Our aircraft also flew privately in what was known as the Red Bull Air Race. These high-energy races hosted some of the best aviators and airplanes in the world. We would uplift guests who were heading out to a nearby lake where the event was being held. We then proceeded to land on the lake and have lunch on the wings of the Albatross. The Red Bull private helicopter would fly overhead, doing loops and rolls as a private air show for our guests. At this time, it was the only civilian helicopter authorized to go upside down on US soil. My exposure to flying at this level with elite talent and intelligence ensured the success of my aviation foundation. With the excitement decibels consistently in the *green* over a two-year period, I decided to invest further in my aviation future.

I enrolled in a professional pilot program, ready to take flying to the next level; it was time to fly jets! Ninety days and $50,000 later, I successfully accumulated all knowledge and passed the practical tests. I obtained all available pilot ratings, including advanced ratings my first time around. Talk about inspired! It was as if my highest powers of comprehension had activated. I couldn't learn fast enough. The momentum of passion and purpose kept me in the dynamic flow. Most time was spent prioritizing the readings and practical knowledge. Both the aeronautical books and the mentorships were equally valuable. I maintained company with the best aviators I could find, asking as many flying questions as came to mind. Since I was the first aviator in my family, I made family with other aviators. Being an aviator meant sharing blood. It was who I was.

As a practical exercise, I was introduced to sensorimotor meditation. We called this chair flying. Chair flying is common practice among pilots. I would sit in a chair and pretend I was sitting on the flight deck of the aircraft. I would imagine the phases of flight and flight scenarios one by one. I would respond to the abnormalities of flight methodically. Chair flying meant putting myself in the feeling state of the real flying experience. From the chair, I repeatedly accomplished flight flows, exactly like I was expected to when I would fly. It meant imagining from the first person. From the seat of the pilot, I was doing everything like it was happening in real time. Sensorimotor meditation would last approximately fourteen days, after which I would be ready for the flight deck. As my imagination muscles grew in fortitude, the airplanes I flew turned into jets, and the jets turned into business jets. The business jets increased in range, and before I knew it, I was piloting business jets around the world.

YOGA AND SEEK

Yoga is infinite. To begin, the path of yoga first reveals itself as an eight-limb system: (1) *yamas* (abstinences), (2) *niyamas* (observances), (3) *asanas* (yoga postures), (4) *pranayama* (breath control), (5) *pratyahara* (withdrawal of the senses), (6) *dharana* (concentration), (7) *dhyana* (meditation), and (8) *samadhi* (absorption). In addition, there are 195 known governing principles called the yoga sutras of Patanjali. These have been handed down mouth to ear until written in ancient sacred texts in approximately 500 BCE.

The yoga language is called Sanskrit. Sanskrit is as magical as yoga itself. Sanskrit words are known to carry so much power that when spoken they have the potential to restore full vision in the practitioner. With this secret knowledge known in yoga circles, it's an honor and a privilege to find oneself with a teacher who can deliver the physical class and asana practice in its original tongue. Practicing yoga thoroughly is like being a chemist inside of our own bodies—continuing to remove the unneeded until arriving in a consciousness of presence. Entry into yoga is a gift.

Being able to hear the knock of my heart during my first class was just enough to attract me further into the mystery of its infinite nature. As a young woman with flying dreams and a desperate need to rid myself of a life lived with the bondage of a negative ego—I let go. I opened my mind to a world of infinity. Yoga was the perfect complement to flying. I could practice in any space my travels took me. I could take yoga with me everywhere. In my seeking, I believe yoga discovered me. I immersed myself in yoga's eight-limb system as well as its sutras while also studying Sanskrit. Yoga was at first something I applied, but then I became the application of its principles.

Organically, the fifth limb of yoga (called pratyahara, the withdrawal of the senses) entered my consciousness. Pratyahara is a magical opening that bridges the gap between external and internal environments. Pratyahara begins with withdrawing from external distractions. The removal of these attachments that no longer serve where we are headed on the illuminated path is a purification process. Like a cosmic-vibrational light healing, pratyahara replenishes the solar plexuses within the body. The removal of what no longer serves our work in the light is very personal to the individual's journey. For me, it was the removal of another layer of toxins. These toxicities were attached to me because of my rejection of connectedness with my source of good. From a separated state, I was deluding myself into a place of needing outside things to be okay. If left in this state, the level of things I needed increased in volume, which led to hoarding and greed. Toxicities could be pretty, shiny things, but only if I allowed those pretty, shiny things to define my wholeness.

We are left to decide for ourselves what will be removed. Our veils of perception are directly proportional to how deep we meet ourselves in attachment. I am attempting to sustainably raise my consciousness, and in order to raise my consciousness, I am taking a personal inventory on items that my senses are stimulated by—specifically those that have been suppressed. First comes the stimulation of the attachment, then the weakening of the spirit in the suppressed state. It then takes extra work to rise back up again, but the wrong habit is formed in the mind. We reach again for the stimulant, and then further suppressing occurs. Self-discipline comes into play with pratyahara, a discipline that is harnessed by allowing our light from within to replace the emptiness we meet from the item being removed.

We continue on to address internal emotions as they arrive: our process is to give our emotions time as we dive deep into this process of emoting. We accept ourselves fully without any desire to leave the feeling ostracized. Feeling something means purifying it. Purification means purging until it's gone. We eventually have enough space for a bridge to form, which will create new neuropathways. This is pratyahara. The stillness of pratyahara carried me, told me to take a seat and meditate. In connecting the outer and inner environments, I began to focus on the air going in and out of my nostrils. In some way, attention to the air connected me to it in a new way altogether—and I became the air. I was consciousness in the air; I could travel consciously—but only as air. Consistently meditating (after asana practice) produced calming results. My awareness in performing due diligence in my meditation practice was at hand. I began to look forward to meditation and riding on the air. My conscious contact with my inner light was regenerating my being. The amount of bliss I experienced after a ten-minute meditation would last the whole day. It also directed the activities of my day in a blissful way. I was practicing yoga whenever the sun came up and sometimes twice daily in light of getting close to a particular pose that required further expansion and flexibility.

The alignment of how to build a yoga pose is complicated but doable across all poses. The longer I could hold the pose and breathe through the strategic twists, I was provided with further insight and a greater sense of humility. So much was here in one single pose. As I went deeper into pratyahara and found that barriers were present, I would enter into a period of fasting when I would only consume wheatgrass juice. Wheatgrass juice is loaded with chlorophyll and was my go-to for many years. Overall, it was a champion in vitamins A, C, and D, as well as being a superfood. There are enough nutrients in wheatgrass to save the planet. My hair, skin, and nails responded to it like flowers in the Garden of Eden. My clinging to food for emotional comfort had vanished. Wheatgrass juice would do the trick on days when I depended solely on my conscious contact with my inner light. Eating vegan assisted entry into meditation with the air. My thoughts were becoming compassionate sailboats in my mind. My senses were transforming from a clinging of *I need* to being *I am*. Up until this point, I only knew imagination meditation. Now, pratyahara added moving breath through my body as a way of turning on my lights. It felt so rejuvenating that I was beyond inspired.

After a beautiful yoga-glow day, I sat on the bedside and began focusing on the air traveling in and out of my nostrils. At first, my mind tried to control the breath, then it tried to control my belly movement, and finally it settled into acceptance. Mentally, I began sending the breath to different locations in the body, a calmness came over me, and I was only three cycles of breath in when all of a sudden—I was in the upper corner of my room spiritually. It was as though I was the breath—the air—and I could travel. I literally was in the upper corner of my room in spirit, but my body was still in the seated position at the foot of my bed. It was as though I had expanded more of my inner light. I squeaked with fear, and immediately I was in my body. *Whoa!* Super amazed, I decided that would be enough for that time. When our consciousness is directed inward toward our inner light, and a withdrawal of our senses is in practice, miraculous meditation journeying becomes available to us.

The spiritual experience of connecting to our light is deeply personal. Our conscious contact expands our light. By giving it our humble attention, a new awareness is born. Our perceptions shift, and our gifts and talents become activated. Once conscious contact is achieved, we can build upon it each time we connect our light to the greater light. Our gifts and talents are light codes. *Light codes are made of numbers and sounds*—numbers and sounds of creation. One yogi can perceive things very differently than another yogi, and the level of understanding and application will vary based on the sincerity of our intention and the efficacy of attainment. I don't have to understand the math fully; we are a young species, and our individualism counts on our light-code activation. The light codes deliver what I need to know in this moment. There are no shortcuts in spiritual experience—the light-code activations are the means upward on the ascension ladder.

Spiritual principles are here to offer us supreme protection in our ascension journey, a protection that is as sustainable as the sun rising. Shortly after this profound experience with the air and meditation, I had a flight manifestation to Berlin, Germany. It was during the winter season. There is no feeling like aviating and navigating the high speed of a business jet across the northern Atlantic Ocean from the United States to the European coast. The international aviation knowledge, and competency, required for a flight in the busiest airspace in the world—is reserved for another tier of pro pilots. The northern lights can be seen as they illuminate a parallel flight course. Adventuring into new cities and countries for the first time with the poise of accomplishment added several inches to becoming human for me.

Crossing the Pond

With nothing but sincere appreciation for my position in life, there I stood at the snowy doorstep of the Jivamukti Yoga studio in Mitte, Berlin. My jet-setting career had taken flight. I was piloting private business jets around the world. Social media was on the rise. It created a channel of inspiration for pilots and other professionals to share their experiences with the world in live time. Instagram offered a quantitative way to stay in touch with friends and mentor young women while flying around the globe. With yoga and flying both occupying my heart equally, I created YOGAIRFORCE as my social media account. This account would accumulate ten thousand followers prior to its dissolution. These followers were the wind beneath my wings. Days before landing anywhere new, my personal protocol was to map out my yoga classes. Interestingly enough, most people only knew me as YOGAIRFORCE. If I crossed anyone following my account in a city around the world, they would recognize me and call me by my social media name: YOGAIRFORCE, my virtual identity.

Any country I jet-set to became an opportunity to collect yoga knowledge in new interpretations of the ancient teachings. Social media presented a platform for research. It made seeking fun. Researching instructors in different cultures, reading bios, and seeking the best yoga gems I could find was a scavenger hunt. The Jivamukti Yoga studio in Berlin had its own app with a logo that was eye-catching. Apps were new for small businesses in the year 2012. Jivamukti's logo followed the golden ratio, such that each number is the sum of the two preceding ones. This formula is found in nature repeatedly, and it mathematically represents life-forms on a cellular level. This wasn't my first interaction with the golden ratio logo, but this was, in fact, my first understanding of Divine proportion. I could now see all the logos that intelligently followed this pattern of geometry. Successful businesses were in their wake. My DNA was responding to the patterns of geometry, and I had drawn this intelligence to me. The simple logo had the power to alter my consciousness. Logos were symbolic of the sounds and numbers of the universe that was inside of me. I was coming to know the One through Divine proportion. Sounds and numbers were its codes.

On the Jivamukti Yoga app, it explained that *jiva* is Sanskrit for living and *mukti* is Sanskrit for liberation. The loose translation is "living liberated," or "being liberated while living." The Sanskrit name stopped me from looking any further. I had found where I would lay my mat while in Berlin. Revolutionary at the time, the Jivamukti Yoga studio housed a vegan cafe. My pratyahara meditation had transported me into some kind of wonderful in this newfound Jiva land. I was already practicing yoga's first-limb yamas. Within the yamas is ahimsa, the non-harming principle. This elevates one's interpretation to the most compassionate lifestyle one can practice. It was the first time I consciously asked myself, *What is my highest truth of living compassionately?* Little did I know, I was asking the right question. That question would be answered infinitely, and as I applied the solutions revealed to me, these solutions that were infinite in nature were built upon.

This would be the beginning of what I know as a sustainable ecosystem on a foundation of truth. Veganism came into my consciousness. It wasn't mainstream at the time. It took work to eat consciously. It meant the sacrifice of a meal if nothing was offered in alignment with my new compassionate contribution. Initially, being vegan meant that (a) I wouldn't eat anything with a face, and (b) I consumed nutrients raw so I could see what I was eating. The contribution of being vegan allowed me to save 1,100 gallons of water, forty-five pounds of grain, thirty square feet of forest, ten pounds of CO_2, and one animal life per day—which cost so little.

I had the anticipation that something phenomenal was about to happen as I entered the Jivamukti Yoga studio for the first time. I read from a simple wooden sign: "Vegan Cafe." The nutritional aroma filled the studio; friends sat around a community table, and fresh air was everywhere. On the hand-painted wall, it read: "Stay, breathe in." I made friends immediately without speaking, and there was a universal kindness that filled the air. Together, we made our way up the stairs to the second floor where the asana practice was held.

Internally, I applauded the hardwood second-floor design, as I knew this was the best engineering for a yoga floor. Taking in the whole room in a 360-degree scan, a spot on the hardwood floor called my name. Selecting spots in yoga rooms has always been a thing for me. The practice is both intimate and metaphysical. These spots just as much choose us as we are called to them. As I rolled out my yoga mat onto the floor, I positively affirmed, *I commit to something greater than myself. I give thanks for the opportunity of continuous growth into Thy highest good.*

That evening in the Jivamukti Yoga studio, I stood tall in *tadasana* (known as mountain pose, where the foundation of our roots and our feet are strong and where energy is drawn up from Mother Earth through our physical form, which activates our light from within). In Europe, the earth felt electric, then the teachers entered the space. There were three teachers, which was new for me. The class began with a third-eye teaching, followed by a corresponding chant, a systematic sequencing of the yoga poses delivered in Sanskrit, and the grand finale meditation.

The asana flow catered to the endocrine system that night. In each movement, I felt a much greater intention surfacing; the Divine presence in the Sanskrit language and the revelations began to unfold in each pose. The concept of projection came into my consciousness. My mind, speaking to me in my own voice, was very convincing as it brought my attention to these yogis flowing around me. The fluidity of the group dynamic was my projection of peace on Earth. Like a grand ballet with a symphony from up above—we flowed together in response to the Sanskrit yoga poses as they were called.

Everyone in the class knew the poses in Sanskrit, and magic was among us. I became acutely aware of everything I was experiencing in my current manifestation, as well as a projection of what I was seeing within myself. The light within was singing, and as a result I was dancing. I was not alone. Others could hear the music, and they were dancing too. We were all dancing together. Synchronized, our class moved through transitions effortlessly, from one pose to the next with the guidance of breathing. The teacher held us in *virabhadrasana III*, airplane pose. My consciousness chimed in: *Every situation, regardless of my view of it, is there to assist me in my ascension.*

Breathe in One, Breathe in Two

I always liked this pose, and I felt strong in it, since it is also known as the airplane-flying pose. Seeing the other yogi airplanes in my periphery manifested the presence to build my pose. The blessing of great reverence was bestowed upon me in this sacred space. I drew my attention to my foundation:

all four corners of my left foot were activated—toes up. Lines of energy drew up from Mother Earth through the roots of my foundation, passing through every limb of my body in all directions. My right leg soared behind me like the rudder of an airplane, controlling rotation all about my vertical axis. The understanding of a 3D plane was present within me. It was so amazing: the rudder behavior was the exact same as it was in an airplane.

The lines of energy drew up and out of me through my arms, and I developed wings! The energy was a bright-white light; laser-type lights made crosses like a woven basket of every color of the rainbow across the studio. The clean windows from floor to ceiling made the snow falling outside touchable. The light bouncing off of the snow and redirecting itself in infinite lines of energy continued to magnify itself. The power of stillness among us as we held our virabhadrasana III pose was profound. It was steady, and we'd all arrived in a sublime nothingness at the exact same moment.

Breathe in Three, Breathe in Four

I lost my stillness by an interruption from my inner voice. It began speaking to me with vigor, saying "fault" and "blame" are out of the window. Instead of things happening to me in a victim state, all things were happening for me: past, present, and future.

Breathe in Five, Garudasana, the Eagle Pose

Slowly, and with control, I slightly bent the standing leg as I brought my air-flying leg forward and wrapped it around my standing left leg without it touching the floor. Now, wrapping my arms (left over right) as much as the length of my arms would allow, I'd done it—an eagle was about to take flight.

We Stay, Breathe in One

I now understood the active role I had in all of my life's events. My mind did a scan of the horrible events of my childhood, the ones I had kept buried. Would I take responsibility for those too? My body reached its melting point. The heat purification within the pose was the point where a greater sense of responsibility and accountability moved through me. Connecting the dots in my mind, I challenged the new information: if this was absolute truth and universal law, then it must apply to everything and every event of my life. There were no exceptions. It either was or it wasn't. Was I ready to take responsibility at this heightened level? Taking responsibility would mean no more blame or fault for those people and those things anymore. No more holding myself hostage because of the stories of my past that I had no control over. My mind played a tape of the stories I told myself: *This isn't happening because I'm a girl. This didn't work because they were just jealous of me. I can't have that because I'm not enough.*

The new level of ascension was there—the key to the invisible door had been delivered. It was taking responsibility for who I was, every single thing. My consciousness continued to clean itself, going through all that I hadn't been willing to take responsibility for in this life. Overwhelmed, I knew I would have to process this over time. My seeking brought me here. This was a great dissolution of ego, even though I hadn't fully understood it with my mind yet.

In my own power and the power of ego, there would have been no way I could have accepted this truth—but next-level ascension was highly desirable, and it was what I had dedicated my life to. Something greater than me was present, and I could hear it clearly with my heart. I couldn't back it with logic in live time. There was no denying the mysterious revelations or the gorgeously pristine clarity. I became curious about the idea of taking responsibility for all that had ever happened to me. So, why was this important? This was the new riddle I was given to decode. What superpower was I to acquire by owning it?

Transitioning from airplane to eagle pose took the cultivation of strength, balance, and *drishti* focus. Drishti is our ability to go within and seek. We seek through our light, allowing our light to connect us with the One Who Has All Power and All Knowledge. Like fingerprints being solely owned by the individual, so too is individualization an intrinsic path to light codes. Light codes illuminate our gifts and talents. Our gifts and talents are unleashed within us, and all the principles of light present themselves for our evolution. In this inner-freedom state, we have the power to take full responsibility. Before, it was more important to be right; now it was essential to be free.

Not one student teetered through this existentially awesome awakening. I silently attributed this to the graceful presence of our three Jivamukti yoga instructors who had come to deliver the euphoric Sanskrit magic that night. I was so grateful and full. We all were.

> *Adho mukha shvanasana*, inhale, hips draw
> back, exhale feet to hands.
> Inhale *ardha uttanasana*, exhale
> *uttanasana*.
> Inhale, look up, reach up, see, pray, exhale
> *anjali* asana.
> *Virabhadrasana III*, right leg.

Stay, Breathe in One, Breathe in Two

What was on the other side of responsibility? Was my vegan diet responsible for this new revelation? Was it the accumulation of a daily commitment to the yoga flow I'd endured, now ten years? Was it these supernatural instructors teaching in unison? Was it this group dynamic of oneness, moving together into peace? Was it the intention I set as I stepped onto my yoga mat before practice? My consciousness revealed good news to these questions. It said: *The other side is here.* Was this the spiritual teaching of the endocrine system?

At the end of our meditation, peace and compassion filled the room in such a richly charged way. No one spoke. Everyone quietly gathered their belongings with a sense of reverence to one another for bringing their presence to such a phenomenal class—and so, we bowed in namaste, then left the otherworldly experience tucked sweetly into our hearts and minds so we could once again wake up and rejoice on another magical day.

CHAPTER 3

THE SPIRITUAL PRINCIPLE OF LOVE

God is our soul mate.

How can you understand something you don't know exists? Our idea of what's possible limits possibilities. I saw what was possible for others, but I held negative beliefs about why they had the good life. I held excuses for why I couldn't have a good life. My "blames and shames" kept me hostage in my own body, living the lie of separation. Like how the shadow of our physical form appears on the ground when the sun is shining—I was a body living in the shadow of who I really was. I was living a parallel course to who I was supposed to be, but I kept missing the true mark because I pulled *all* my power from outside of myself. Pity.

The spiritual principle of truthfulness began to build upon itself. My first introduction to truthfulness was surrendering *the lie* that I was separate from my source of good. To know this was one thing, but to put my connectedness into action was another. Claiming my connectedness meant taking responsibility for the story I operated from, and the lies I used to cover the original lie that was rooted in *less than* existence. I can never see your fullness if I myself believe I am not full. I can only see what I believe. I project my beliefs onto others, and I attract the circumstances that mirror my beliefs. It was time to take responsibility for the content of my character. Who was I when nobody was looking? What did I believe? Not what I thought I believed—but my actions. Did they add up? As I became ready, the twelve steps of recovery appeared. The invisible door to the next transformational process was right in front of me. The twelve steps of recovery would bring all of me to the light.

The twelve steps are a system that is spiritual in nature when practiced as a way of life. They carry the promise of expelling the obsession with "filling in the blanks with addiction," making the practitioner restored to original condition. The primary mission of the twelve steps is for the practitioner to develop a relationship with the One. The original text of the twelve steps was published in 1939 in *Alcoholics Anonymous: The Big Book*. It was recognized by the US Library of Congress as one of the eighty-eight most influential books to shape America.

What did I need freedom from? In my seeking of a higher understanding of greater awareness, my attention was directed to the suppression of my consciousness. Suppressing was the opposite of what I was trying to achieve. Two questions came to mind: (1) In what ways was I suppressing myself? (2) What was I suppressing so deeply within myself? If I could alleviate the suppressors, then I could get to the root of what I was suppressing *and* take responsibility for it. It seemed simple at first.

Alcohol was at the top of my suppressor list. I looked back at my history of alcohol. It was an important part of everything, from as far back as I could remember. It was interwoven into the culture of my family, my work, and my relationships. Alcohol was my solution to holidays, wins, loses, and five o'clock happy hours. Alcohol was the theme of every holiday and event, which was deeply imprinted into my understanding of social contracts. It was the reward for achievements. It was the perfect pairing for brunch, shopping, and lunch. It was what social dinners were all about. Alcohol was an excuse in and of itself.

> Definition: Alcohol slows down and inhibits neurotransmitters.

Yikes!

> It is obtained by the hydration of gas.

Geez!

Had I blindly bought into drinking as a form of gas that was making me mentally defective? I was a daily drinker, and it had to stop. The connection I was experiencing with my inner light had taken precedence. My desire to have more of these truth principles present themselves through my consciousness was rising. On my own power, I decided alcohol would go away. This lasted a few days, then I would find myself in some predicament where I was drinking again. I would recommit to stopping—but again, I would start drinking. I upped the ante on my workout routine. This had seemed to work in the past—but then I would start drinking again and again. Despite how strong my will was to stop, even adding in daily saunas to my workout routine, the drinking episodes continued.

From the time I became aware that drinking alcohol was inhibiting my brain function, which was thereby inhibiting my ability to connect with the One, I found it virtually impossible to individualize. Stopping for good and for all made for a grueling four months. During this four-month period, I attempted all kinds of self-control with alcohol. In the morning, I'd make a goal not to drink for that day. The goal itself suggested I may not succeed. The goal made it far-fetched in my mind. The goal rejected who I was. Setting the goal took me out of the present and furthered my idea of not measuring up. That one seed of doubt would engulf me.

One night, I set out to prove to myself that I could have only one drink and then go home. That night, I was removed from the restaurant altogether for drinking too much. From my state of drunk consciousness, everything was okay. The response from others proved to be very different. In the mornings, the devastating defeat would settle in, so I would begin again with a new plan—a two-mile run, the sauna, the yoga— then the insidious thought would arise, and I was weakened in my will and solar plexus. I would try morning and afternoon yoga in the same day; surely that would work and kick me off the booze, right? The time in between the drinking was closing in on me. I tried going back to what it was like before I committed to stopping alcohol—but I couldn't. Was my commitment that strong? I couldn't go back, I couldn't go forward, I couldn't stop. It had my mind. It had my ego. It had my will. Haunted by what I could not deny, the morning came with a solution to ask for help. To the heavens, I raised my arms and shouted:

"IIIIII . . . NEEEED . . . HELP!!!!!"

One afternoon, after my yoga practice, I realized that even the yoga bliss was fleeting. While resisting in my body, mind, and spirit—the dreaded walk home of six city blocks was filled with alcohol vendors. God help me. I slowly gathered my belongings—black sheepskin boots beneath a knee-length wool coat, my scarf noosed around my neck—wishing to numb the throat chakra in a way that would make me disappear. I was dressing for my death. To drink was to die, and I was a dead man walking. I lifted my eyes ever so slightly; this couldn't be God's will. The owner of the studio approached me. I felt a wisp of air move through all of my winter garments. In a confused state, I met his eyes. On the darkest night of my soul, I spotted blue speckles in his eyes that were captivating. In a simple way, he asked, "How are you?"

Silence. Thirty seconds of silence expanded between us. My mind traversed the extensions of what I was about to say. Normally, I would liven up, like I was about to go onstage and deliver a speech. Yet I couldn't bring forth the breath to lie about how I was doing. In my mind, I ran through the good things: flying, yoga, and the amazing cities and countries my jet-setting lifestyle afforded me. This was my programmed response to life. My response to life was predicated on my actions. It was predicated on what I had done, but never on my being. *How am I?*

His words replayed in my mind while penetrating my entire being. *How are you?* Something about his presence made the simplest of words meaningful. I could both hear the words and experience the sincerity of their concern. This couldn't have been the first time I heard those words; however, my access to the spiritual experience had begun. This individual was carrying the spiritual experience, and when he spoke, the message was delivered. I couldn't quite put my finger on the thing within him captivating me. I was in the presence of something great, and it was beyond human form. My physical body was exhausted from the daily buildups and routine nightly teardowns. The regenerative nature of being a youth hid a lot. The invincible nature of youth and how I could bounce back from intoxicating events kept me in denial of the hopeless state of mental obsession. I blended into the mediocrity of life by making my hair, my skin, and my wardrobe look "pretty." I moved, became something new, but these behaviors rooted in separateness from God kept me spiritually bankrupt, which meant emotionally ill. The emotional illness would present itself in my physical body soon enough. The daily dry saunas for hours on end used as a way to detoxify the alcoholic toxins within my body led to the removal of the inner lining of my intestines. I began to pass blood in my stool. It would still take another eighteen months of denial and refusing to see before I accepted the twelve-step program to recovery. The hopeless condition was revealed in my vicious cycle of bondage of self. I was branded with changing external things to be okay. How invincible can one be if every time the wind blows, you are affected by it? A further external change would characterize my ignorance of arrogance.

But that was then, before I committed to stopping alcohol. My commitment had somehow come true, and I was being held to sobriety. My emotional body had failed to develop due to an inability to find real solutions in life outside of alcohol. My soul body had somehow been traded to the underworld by self-rejecting who I am and thereby making alcohol my God. Anything in my life that came before God was lost. There are only two wills in the world: human will and God's will. Every time I drank, I was giving up my human will to align with God and instead yielding to the dark force of the drink. Every time I drank, I was suppressing the God consciousness within myself. Every time I drank, I was weakened and susceptible to entities of the dark forces. A drink meant being the host of my ego. An ego that went outside of itself and assigned power to people, places, and things. In this state of confusion, I couldn't differentiate between what was true and false. I was shadowing real life. I remained outside spiritual law. I had no access to my God consciousness. A drink meant all my invisible means of support would vanish. I was at the mercy of dark forces.

The time in between the drinks was no better. With a mind subdued and managed by alcohol, my sober hours consisted of being enslaved to a mind that talked to me in my own voice and was very convincing. When it spoke, I listened. When it spoke with greater intensity, I not only listened but acted. Whatever it wanted to do, we did. The loudest thoughts took priority. My soul body was not within reach with this vicious cycle in motion. The action of giving my will up to dark forces by suppressing what I had come to know as the suffering of life was the only way of life I had known. A weakened will makes people, places, and things its God. It is literally self-rejecting its God consciousness and saying, *No, thank you*, to the miracle of alignment with God. The trance of separateness only allowed for manifestations from the default of separateness. Life was responding to my lie, and it all appeared so real. To get to *the truth* that *I am* connected to God, that I carry God within my humanoid system, *and* it is the "Father's good pleasure to give you the Kingdom" (Luke 12:32) took time.

The owner of the yoga studio that day was also the teacher, and so I began to shed tears. The teacher's presence meant everything to me. I felt I could safely share what was happening to me, so I did. Ironically, the yoga studio owner had twenty-five years of sobriety and was a trusted servant in the twelve steps of recovery—making the crossing of our paths highly synchronistic. The timing of my answered prayer was almost immediate. It had been such a loaded question: *How are you?*

The timing of my request, the location of the answer, and by whom it was delivered made those simple words "how are you" likened to the bow, the arrow, and the bull's-eye; they were steadfast and immovable. Beyond this, the teacher was saying: *I'm here to help.* We innately know when we are in a safe place, facing kindness, experiencing compassion, and in the presence of love. This was my introduction to the spiritual family of Alcoholics Anonymous, where I would practice the twelve steps of recovery as a way of life. The twelve steps of recovery would teach me how to align my human will with Thine will. December 17, 2014, would be the first day of a new life without alcohol for good and for all, and so—it was.

ILLUSTRATION OF CONNECTING TO OUR SOUL MATE

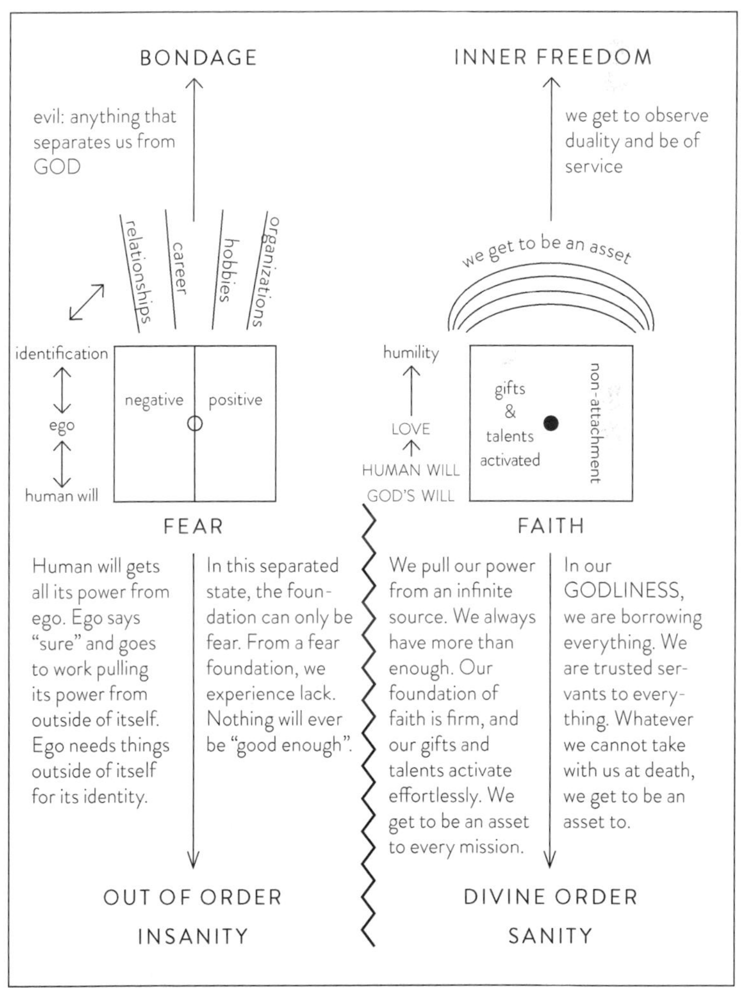

Now with the suppressors gone, it was time to go deeper into what I was suppressing. The heavy trauma from my childhood was rearing its ugly head. I was to do my very best to transmute the pain. Transmuting pain is the process of replacing the lower energy with the higher-energy self. Instead of acting out of the pain body, we choose a sustainable way to channel it. At this point, we get to choose to go to our inner lights for purification. Transmuting pain is a *God-only* healing. Somehow, in my deeper knowing, I knew God would be the only one who could understand and would be the only one who could heal this trauma from within. It was interesting how becoming completely abstinent from suppressors was allowing these traumas (which were responsible for my old ideas of separateness) to surface. They were surfacing uninvited like a marching band from far off drawing closer. First, I only heard a beat every day or so, then a couple of beats in the day, then the beats and the stomping, then the entire band getting closer and closer until they were passing right by me. It was a demanding presence, to say the least: these loud cymbals clanging, percussionists paddling and pounding, horns screeching and blowing, and heavy boots systematically marching.

Suppressing my consciousness came to a screeching halt. I was being guided into the transcendence of all things no longer serving my highest good. My emotional body was at large. I stood ready to overcome that which was blocking it from the sunlight of the Spirit. This was new knowledge. I had no idea life was responding to my erroneous core beliefs. I had no idea I thought from my beliefs. I had no ideas of my own. Unbeknownst to me, I had the ideas I'd adopted in my formative years being raised outside of the spiritual experience. Truly, I never thought about it. I was too busy enduring life with no choice. I lived by the proverbial phrase: "When life gives you lemons, make lemonade." I was the most optimistic person I knew. Optimism was my solution for the misfortune of life.

I had reentered my journey of childhood. Emotionally, I was eight years old. This was the age when deeply disturbing events happened in my life. My young mind was wounded without resolution. Now, in the fourth step of the twelve-step recovery program, I was to make a searching and fearless moral inventory of myself. This first time around with the fourth step, I didn't have too much searching to do. The inventory of trauma was a marching band emerging from my consciousness. It was time to face the music. The fourth step of Alcoholics Anonymous states: "Made a searching and fearless moral inventory of ourselves." Here, I would learn how to write out my inventory with a trusted servant of the twelve-step program. This trusted servant would freely pass on fourth-step sacred knowledge to me. I would then be expected to practice the fourth step as a way of life until it was my turn to pass it on to those whom I would serve for fun and for free. "For fun and for free" meant that I would carry the message of God in such a way that the receiver could never repay me. The continuance of passing it on would afford the privilege of continuing in the spiritual experience. The gift of fourth-step strategic journaling is that it allows you to become masterful in being freed from the deadly bondages of self. The "bondage of self" manifested as a way to weave a pattern of resistance from exposing the untreated wounds. The bonds of self were years of bandages. The bonds of self were the only way I knew how to protect myself as I was unaware of a spiritual experience and spiritual principles that produce a cure. As the devastating memories arose, so too did the anger associated with them. Once the anger subsided, I could then begin to feel the deep sorrow of a broken heart. The admission of complete defeat over this process with a sincerity of heart was the magic. The strategic journaling of the fourth step opened the door to my emotional body. I became more *aware* of my deep-seated wounds. I wrote down all of it: who I was upset with, what had happened, the parts of my emotional body (self-esteem, pride, personal relations, finances, sexual relations) that were affected by these excruciating events. I wrote it all out. I wrote like my life depended upon it, because it did. Awareness was essential to uncovering this part of me that desperately needed to be heard. Unlike before, where my personality was relentless in making lemonade with the lemons of life, I now had the power to let go, feel, and accept myself exactly as I was in the moment. This was altogether different. The power to write was unusual. I was experiencing courage. This was uncharted territory. I had the strength to write how I *really* felt in the face of suffering and the distress of a broken heart. I kept reminding myself all of this was a gift. I persisted in gratitude. In gratitude, I was able to cuddle the pain and experience the hurt with full equanimity. I reminded myself that awareness was a gift of *being* through *feeling*. I had never given myself permission to be with the emotional shock of gloom-ridden events. I was embarrassed and shameful for experiencing my childhood. My childhood perception was that I was responsible, I was the reason the giants (those persons that towered over us as children, the authority figures) in my life were maladjusted to life. In my childhood mind, feeling hopeless, I thought it was all my fault. I felt responsible for my broken family. I was powerless over their decision-making. My moral inventory was taking me to school. My part was to allow it to happen and to be thorough in my writing. My part was to be present in my feelings. Courageously, my greatest internal mysteries were being solved.

The initial fourth step was a cleansing of my consciousness from eight years old up until the present, thirty-five years old. Twenty-seven years of thorough cleansing was happening *for* me. The consciousness entering my awareness was revealing a new perspective. The way I looked at things began to change. Every circumstance was happening for my spiritual awakening to take place. My soul had taken the most direct path, attracted the most appropriate people, at the most Divine time. I envisioned the characters in the theater of life I was seeing removing their mask and taking a bow, like at the end of a theatrical performance. Plot Twist!

A specific resentment I had, for which I learned to *casually weather its storm*, would be the turning point in my fourth-step inventory process. The person I felt resentful toward was a family member. This wound was buried so deep that I kept fooling myself it wasn't a big deal. I had been brainwashed to think it wasn't a big deal. The trauma placed me in my favorite T-shirt as a child. This was a loving thought. My favorite T-shirt symbolized freedom. I wore it every day after elementary school. As soon as I got home, I would change into my favorite T-shirt and go play outside. The T-shirt was cotton, and I loved the way it felt on my skin. In this T-shirt, I did things I loved. As I was experiencing these loving memories, the movie in my head took a dark turn. My attention went to the giants (adults) that surrounded me. I began to see their struggles. The things the giants would say to each other and how they interacted with each other. I saw my uncle. He wore a football jersey that made him appear healthy and admirable. He was super tall and liked by the family from my perception. My uncle made friends with me as a child. He was a trusted uncle because he showed me new things and made me feel special. However, he was spiritually sick. He began abusing his position of *trusted uncle* by stealing the innocence and purity of my body. For my developmental mind, this was an infringement of wholeness, an act of abuse, a rape of my mind. The abandonment settled in as I wrote it all down. The rage poured out of me and onto the paper. How could this ever be OK? I knew in my eight-year-old mind that what he was doing with me was wrong, but I was made to believe it was right behavior. I believed in the image of him. In my little mind, he had authority. Trying to differentiate between what was true and false was very confusing as a child. Who could I trust? Anyone? The level of coping required at that moment with Earth's hazardous people was unbearable.

The disappointment family members expressed toward me for inconveniencing them when I attempted to share what was happening to me. The doubtful looks from family members as they questioned my integrity. The nuisance I had become to my schoolteachers as they acted like I had given them a piece of information I should have kept to myself. The debate over the course to take in everyone else's best interests while never consulting me. The negative core beliefs I adopted in my mind from that one event were tremendous. This one event with its rippling effect changed the course of my reliance from that point forward. It changed my beliefs about everything. The feelings of being cheated were unbearable. My heart was now in sync with the anatomy of an existential drumbeat. I hadn't given this experience my full presence until now, at thirty-five years old. As an eight-year-old, the vast nature of spiritual know-how was out of reach. The sexual exploitation of my childhood was at hand. Indirectly, the subsequent tragedies linked to this one event replayed in my mind. The desire for justifiable revenge came to the surface, and my writing was paced with grace. Pause. Feel. Breathe.

In the fourth step, pain was the touchstone of growth. I had days of total meltdown and deep despair. The depressed emotions were being lifted in a calm and gentle way. There was conditional protection in the spiritual experience with application of the spiritual tools (honesty, hope, faith, strength, courage, perseverance and so many more) as long as I continued my work on the altruistic plane. I could see so clearly now how I projected years of my discomfort onto the canvas of life. My ill feelings manifested in my human experience. There was always this "ick" element in every chapter of my life. The "ick" would sour the entire chapter. The "ick" would be an annihilation of all good things in every chapter of my life. The cycle of my "ick" was clear (through the adoption of my consciousness), but never until now did I have the POWER to overcome it. Never, until now, did I have the spiritual-tool knowledge and enough self-love to appropriate right action. At the end of each chapter was an explosion, not a transition. Having justice and being justified are not the same thing. From the agony of being justified, I just let go. I was hurt, and hurt people *hurt people.*

Fearlessly, I wrote out what happened, leaving nothing out. Like a child being taught to tie their shoelaces by a loved one, there she was, little Amielle, at the mercy of an uncle who felt entitled to my little eight-year-old body. He'd been a trusted family member, an authority figure, one whom I'd looked up to and idolized as a child. He'd even worn one of those football jackets with all the lettering; I remembered the sight of it. Then I remembered his predatory sickness, demonstrated on me as a way for him to have an orgasm at his pleasure. Where was everyone else when this was happening? How could my parents not know this was happening? How could this sickness ever be removed from me completely?

Ughhhhhhhh!

My part was to allow myself to feel this uncomfortable trauma in the presence of God by inviting God into my writing, inviting God into my pain, and accepting it all with the power of grace. I had become willing to release these faulty core beliefs, these behaviors that were being cast out by God's grace. My writing brought me into the fetal position, lying sideways on my bed. I was in a state of lock, shock, and barrel, lying completely naked—guts exposed from an emotional bomb that had just gone off. It was as though I lay in the middle of the street while the marching band observed my agony, all the while playing louder and unabashedly continuing forward.

The infringement on my developing eight-year-old mind was devastating. Disgusted and full of rage, I scribbled heatedly across the page. In writing it out, I was giving it to God. Writing it out was a sustainable way of *acceptance* through the positive channel of *truthfulness.* The intuitive thought arrived: *evil exists in the world.* I wanted a sobriety that could go through anything. I wanted a sobriety in the spiritual experience. *God, don't let anything get in the way of my spiritual awakening.* I had to become willing to feel it, and be with it with God.

In the third part of the fourth step, I would become rigorously honest with how this event had *affected* me. My self-esteem had been greatly affected, due to feeling shame and guilt in front of my friends. This amplified the fear of having my peers find out what was happening *to* me. My pride was greatly affected, due to worrying about what others would say or think about me. My ambition was greatly affected, due to living in a state of insecurity that was inhibiting my ability to follow my dreams. My security was affected, due to believing that the people I looked up to and thought I could trust weren't protecting me. My personal relations were affected, due to not being able to trust the strongest personal relations an eight-year-old could have: her parents. My sexual relations were affected, due to being shown sex in an impure way, which had me believing that sex meant nothing to me other than exploitation. And finally, my pocketbook had been affected, because I thought all I was, *was* a body—and this body was my power—which was my true source of income. Cursed with a thousand forms of fear, I continued to write. The marching band was still playing but had stopped marching. The horn section played loudest, and the trumpets screamed all at once.

Finally, the fourth part of the fourth step was here. The strategic journaling had taken several months. The final part had arrived. Here, I was asked to take responsibility for my part in the resentment. Did I have a part? The answer was no at the surface level. For I was just a child, powerless over what had happened. I did, however, have a part in my "justified behaviors" that followed this event. All of these behaviors were rooted in separateness from God. This was the faulty foundation upon which my entire life was built. I believed I was responsible for all the good in my life. Due to the amount of work required for the simplest of things, when I did accomplish something, my level of entitlement was out of the park. I was in a constant state of defending a life that was happening *to* me. I had fallen prey to sweet revenge. In a moment of clarity, my consciousness recited that Martin Luther King Jr. quote: "Hate cannot drive out hate; only *love* can do that" (emphasis mine). I smiled. I began seeking a higher love in my heart and through meditation. Agape love. Moments of good thoughts began to flow into my mind, and it was refreshing. Discussing the fourth column with a trusted servant would close the loop. By discussing it with a trusted servant, I had fulfilled the requirement of the fourth step. This is when the trusted servant with more sober time than I would shed light on the fact: "Our problems arise out of ourselves" (*Alcoholics Anonymous*). *Gulp.*

I was responsible for cultivating Divine indifference for being infected by sick people. I wasn't to agree *it* was *in any way* God's will, but rather harness higher love towards the wound and suffering it manifested, placing me in a state of Divine neutrality (acknowledgement yet unaffectedness). In this way, I could be useful to others through real empathy. I was learning true empowerment by way of opening myself to higher love. The receiving of higher love became possible. The softening to receive was at hand. I was becoming that which I was receiving, higher love. I was being pulled from the gates of victimhood into a new freedom and new happiness. This I had never before experienced.

The decisions I made from eight years of age until now, I was being held accountable for in a kind and gentle manner. WOW. I had been creating it all. I am creating it all. My problems were of my own making. Yes, the false had appeared real. I had tangible results to prove these things that happened to me, but *they all* were a by-product of the belief of my separation from God. As long as I held that faulty belief in my mind, I would continue to manifest outside of the grace of spiritual principles. Another word for Spirit is "God." Another word for principle is "law." Spiritual principles are God's law. A law I didn't even know existed before reclaiming my consciousness by way of being clean and sober.

The trusted servant and I completed one spiritual step at a time. In the completion of a spiritual step, the spiritual experience of God's promises came true. Being aligned with God's law brought forth serenity and peace. We are not alone. "For where two or more are gathered in my name, there I am in the midst of them" (Matthew 18:20). In the fourth column of the fourth step, I became willing to transcend the pain with my God consciousness. I was able to observe the suffering of all elements arising out of myself, and to finally give it all to God in the presence of the trusted servant. The disgusting, angry, and filthy feelings were being lifted by a power greater than myself. This spiritual tool being handed down to me called my soul from deep hibernation into its right-sized seat. The metamorphosis of being bound by external power, the bondage of self, was in its final stage. The spiritual transformation was in process. I was becoming.

The anger lifted from every cell within my body. The embarrassment began to vanish. The fear was uprooted and expelled, from root to branch, *gone*. Rest was my friend. I lay in rest for many days undisturbed. The trauma was dissipating like a heavy rain cloud. Calling upon God was my superpower. For the first time, I allowed people to care for me. These people were members of the fellowship of Alcoholics Anonymous. They did so *for fun and for free*. There were no strings attached. It wasn't tit for tat. Their only aim was to be helpful. When I could, I would add any residual anger to paper. In this fourth step of healing, I became aware that rape is a crime of violence, not of sexuality. We are wired to know what is inherently right, and at the age of eight, I knew it was wrong, despite having no access to proper healing.

Each day, I was healing both one breath at a time and one moment at a time. Two weeks passed, and like a virus leaving the body, I began to gain new strength and new freedom. Finally, the past and future versions of myself aligned with me in the present. God's grace whipped around me. I rose out of my sickened state and took a magnificent inhale. My breath had depth. No one was around to see it all dissipate. There was no inner fight and no outer flight. The detailed memories came up, up and away like a hot-air balloon catching the wind. The cleansing illuminated my soul. I prayed in continual whispers to God.

Thank you, God. Thank you, God. Thank you, God. Thank you, God.

When the transformation was complete, I went straight to the mirror and looked myself right in the eyes. *Who are you?* I *loved* what I saw. I truly thought, *I have a chance!* A new sense of worthiness had flooded into that hole of pain and the void that I had tried to fill so many times with outside resources, both good and bad. All I could experience in that moment was forgiveness. As the forgiveness grew within me, I felt humility for life. The wound, the piercing of my mind by evil, was brought to the light, purified, and forgiven. God and me, we were one. My truest soul mate was revealed. A supernatural *love* filled my wounds with immeasurable beauty. I returned to the purity of innocence fully, which gave me the power to freely forgive.

These traumatic events of the past were not *who I was.* These traumas were past tense; they were a story I told myself and, consequently, had bound myself to. A thought surfaced: *The only thing worse than being wrong is staying wrong.* My interpretation of these events had driven my life, leaving me to live up to the expectations of *the lie.* My entire life was a representation of overcompensating for this lie. My ego needed this story to survive, it needed the lie. Alcohol had kept me in this misunderstanding for twenty-seven years. My human will, with its own power, gave direction to my ego, which was pulling its power from the things outside of myself. This was the cycle of defeat: *the hopeless condition revealed.*

CONNECTING HEAVEN AND EARTH RIGHT NOW

A new connectedness with God was being born from within consciousness. The foundation of my old belief system was crumbling in the face of God. Fear was transformed into faith. I would speak a new language, not a cultural-based language but the words of God. Access to a new vocabulary was granted with words to compliment the miracle of life, the miracle of God. Any human being connected to their godliness is experiencing the mind of God by way of living in the heart of God. I was to "walk by faith now, not by sight" (2 Corinthians 5:7). This state of mind, the mind of God, transformed *I have to* into *I get to.* The inner faith foundation drew upon an infinite source, and the feelings of running out of money, running out of time, and overall limited supply vanished. The inner faith foundation was sound, stable, steadfast, and immovable. The trust fund of others I once envied and judged became clear. I became aware that a trust fund is *the source of good* that is readily available to all of us in the mind of God. It was my Divine right to draw upon it as I wished. The psychic change came with a trust fund. I could draw upon it as much as I wanted, when I wanted, and how I wanted. My trust fund was a function of the foundation of faith that filled my heart like never before.

Grace. Grace. Grace.
Love. Love. Love.
Thank you.
Thank you, God.

This is what it means to be sane. Sanity is going inside of myself and tapping my unlimited inner resource. What was left of my ego took a back seat to what was unfolding in my God consciousness. What was blossoming inside of me was much bigger than what was outside of me. There was only surrender. One deep breath of the spiritual awakening was all it took to increase my willingness to do whatever was necessary to keep this thing flowing through me. I could see the new alignment taking place. I could see a tree of life growing from the foundation of my faith. It was intertwined like a helix of DNA. My God-given talents and gifts activated. My ego ultimately dissolved into nothingness, for it had served its purpose. The ego's purpose was to guide the soul body into the spiritual awakening. God's agape love was in every nanoparticle of what was happening within me and *for* me now. God's agape love was streaming out of me and into all of my affairs as pure kindness. God's agape love was beyond anything I had ever imagined. God's agape love was healing and restoring me to my original condition. God's agape love was having its way with me, and I was never the same.

HOW DO YOU KNOW IF YOU ARE SERVING THE EGO?

When I first searched and researched higher consciousness with a mind free of self, it was revealed as a greater awareness (of life). With the embodiment of greater awareness, privilege of life was afforded to me. Full self-reliance became possible.

Greater awareness afforded observation of duality in life (cause and effect). Observation of duality was the act of rising above ordinary existence in consciousness in order to observe the good and evil within myself. Whatever I could solve within my own mystery allowed me to assist others in that same mystery. I would only be able to assist at the level at which I met my own mystery. I wanted to assist. This was exciting. The next revelation of higher consciousness was my responsibility to tap my inner resource (inner light), bringing forth an innate ability to manifest consciously. Prior to the psychic change, I was responding to life in a habitual way. I had been manifesting by the default of negative core beliefs. Now, I had a choice. The final element of higher consciousness meant having the intelligence to connect with the Creator of All Creation. In doing so, I would continue to accept greater responsibility as *its* consciousness revealed to me where I could further clean my consciousness. I was responsible for the consciousness I was carrying, and as I cleaned it with the greater consciousness of all of creation, I had a direct experience with God. Ascending into higher consciousness also meant connecting to other intelligent beings here and in our galaxy. Having access to higher consciousness allowed the becoming of the full human. The full human meant mastering my light and, in doing so, experiencing greater portions of the grace of God's law.

The dawn of my spiritual awakening made clear human suffering. So many suffered from the lie of separateness from God. Humans were gravely handicapped by believing God was something outside of themselves. This kept humans outside of the grace of God's law. My personal experience proved the separated state to be deadly. I was dying from being separated from God's law. My human will had gotten all of its fuel from the ego (which was the only power available on my own power). The ego pulls all of its power from its identification with people, places, and things (like a career, a relationship, a hobby, etc.). *I am a pilot* is a powerful proclamation and absolutely beautiful, but when this is *who I think I am* at the core level, then I work for *the pilot* and not for God. I'd been pulling my power from *the pilot* (and everything that came with the lifestyle of a pilot), and inevitably serving a false master! While I had worldly success in flying, the work was serving the self and therefore unusable in the eternal journey. Only the work done on the altruistic plane can be carried with us when we depart our human experience. I spent so much time perfecting the skills of flight, and never once did I ask God, *How can I use these flying skills for your Great Work? How can these flying skills touch the hearts, the minds, and the beautiful actions of 7.5 billion people?* These were the kinds of questions becoming available to me in the psychic change. The shadowing of my *true self* had passed over. The full activation of my gifts and talents was now possible.

GOD'S PILOT REPORTING FOR DUTY!

The very nature of being separated produced a "lack consciousness." Lack consciousness is the consciousness of "there isn't enough." There isn't enough is the physical manifestation of "I am not enough." This was the very opposite of "love consciousness." The ego then went to work producing more (hence commanding me to do more), and off I went. Another accolade, another relationship, another "fill in the blank"— whatever the taste of the ego was at that particular moment that needed to be appeased. Prior to the psychic change, I was a physical body with thoughts, and my thoughts were my god. When my thoughts had intensity, I acted faster, serving my self-centeredness, otherwise referred to as an ego-driven life.

Willingness to raise one's consciousness is the beginning of correct order, of Divine order. Divine order is the proper use of human will in alignment with spiritual connectedness. Divine order is being in alignment with the Divine nature of both my soul body and spirit body. The connectedness is with the One Who Has All Power and All Knowledge. The human will aligned with the will of God is called *seating the soul*. This process is making a conscious decision to meditate on the centermost point of our minds. The centermost point of our brain is known as the mind's eye. We see a light and focus on this light until the light portal opens to us. Once the portal is open, we can ascend into the higher self and experience connection with the One Who Has All Power and All Knowledge. Our higher consciousness experience has begun. In our meditation practice, regeneration becomes possible. We are led by *the power of God* to clean our consciousness in precise ways. The guidance weighs on our consciousness, and we intuitively know what needs to be done. In this way, the human will is pulling all of its power from the One—and everything changes.

By Divine design, life shows up to *free up* what has been *bound up*, and once complete, we can *suit up and show up*. Serving our Divine life contracts is at hand. Don't miss your life! On Earth, we find ourselves in the situations and circumstances that best serve the cultivation of our relationship with God. The spiritual shift of the psychic change makes serving God accessible to all. Our gifts and talents activate in serving our Divine life contracts. In God's grace, we come to know this wholeheartedly. Our broken hearts are healed by God. We get to be free from the confines of what we think *we ought to be* and we get to be *who we are*.

The evolution of the ego is set up into thirds: the first third of life is the development of the ego, the second is the execution, and the third is the dissolution. If we miss the mark entirely in the third part and never discover our connection to the One, then our journey leads us to some devastating moment, or a series of devastating moments, where we are brought to our knees in surrender by either outside forces or physical ailments. Whatever happens in life bringing us to this magical point of desperation, it will be a problem only God can solve. We then call upon Spirit by necessity. Hopefully at this point, we can move into a transition of what is truly important. We can *accept* our Divine life contract. Divine life contracts are put into place by an infinite intelligence for each soul body. They are unique to an individual soul, and only that soul can fulfill its contract. An understanding of the psychic change is demonstrated when we let go of attachments. When we internalize the spiritual fact that only our work on the altruistic plane counts in our eternal journey. Anything designed by the ego (to support the ego) will be forgotten. In our psychic change transitions, there is oftentimes a struggle, a grieving of the old self, but self-determination to align with our Divine life contracts must always win.

The prolonging of forward movement once Spirit has spoken equals suffering. If we can't let go, then we are dragged and mangled by our resistance to the responsibility of serving our Divine life contract. Grieving while connected to the heart of God is a healthy process associated with the loss of our old selves. Accepting the responsibility of our Divine life contracts translates as inner freedom—a freedom from within that is sustainable. Inner freedom illuminates the heart mind, a mind taking its direction from love consciousness. Breaking free from the bondage of ego is a victory. Inner freedom opens us to the field of infinite possibilities. In this fulfilled state, the soul of God is in union with its creator. God is our soul mate. The ego has served its purpose in the evolution of our consciousness. The ego dissipates: this is what it means to be "right-sized," and the ego evaporates. There is no regret or morbid reflection about the previous life with ego; instead, there is humor and humility. The psychic change produces the dawn of an ever-increasing spiritual awakening where spiritual principles become available to us in God's law. Spiritual principles are present tense, and in the moment of appropriation, they produce a cure. Our *mastery of light practice* begins. Our new way of life and dependence upon God is practiced by going within ourselves. As we do this, the activation of our light codes with the spiritual principles is revealed. Light codes are the numbers and sounds of God. God and *love* have no opposite. God decides when the consciousness we are carrying is ready—and, when all the stars align, we proceed to the next level in the ascension process.

PART II

CHAPTER 4

OUT OF THE FOG

Godshots on the house!

It had been nineteen months of continuous sobriety while working the twelve steps of recovery. I was on the nineteenth day of a Master of Light meditation practice. This was a practice that organically unfolded itself while I was observing the light in the centermost point of my heart, then imagining a helix of light from my heart to my mind. In this way, love consciousness would lead the light in my mind. My focus on this schematic, free of thoughts, opened a portal of light in my consciousness. I then was present within the portal of light and could experience the presence of light in all things. This was how I received the "hidden manna" (Revelation 2:17). Hidden manna is symbolic for *the means and the ways* of the Master of Light. Receiving the hidden manna was necessary for the receiving and sustainability of all things eternal. It nurtured my human experience beyond measure. The Master of Light fulfilled my soul's salvation as well. I was completely dependent upon it for good and for all.

Springing from an AA meeting I regularly attended called "Out of the Fog," I spotted piercing white clouds in the livening blue sky. In a louder-than-normal voice, I projected: "It's a gorgeous day! *Wow!*" My words caught the attention of whoever was around. In a city, one can shout out into midair, anything goes. Feeling the power of my previous decision, I projected my voice a bit louder and further: "Look at those white puffy clouds perfectly suspended in midair. *Wow!*" Now, I had the attention and smiles of people passing by me. I elongated my back body with a deep breath, and with perfect poise, feeling unbelievably comfortable in my skin, eyes first, I looked *up* to the heavens. My head followed next (where the eyes go, the body follows), upward toward the heavens. The curvature of the whole planet felt like a dome of serenity—a canopy of absolute peace wrapped around our planet, our home. My heart surrendered reverence in each cardinal direction: North, I bowed. East, I bowed. South, I bowed. West, I bowed. I had made a full clockwise circle, bowing to each direction, and felt like I was designed to do this. Turning in a clockwise circle felt like winding a watch for it to start. I took the deepest inhale and felt an abundance of gratitude for the air molecules traveling into my lungs. "*Wow!* Air molecules. Life. *Wow!*" Right away, feeling an elated sense of sincere appreciation, my connection to the air delivered the utmost admiration for life. "Life. *Wow! I am one.*" I suddenly became hyperaware of the volume of space that was carrying the air that was allowing for life *within me* and *in everything else. I am connected. I am alive. I am Divine. I am here now.* These were the thoughts coming through my consciousness and out of my mouth. *"I am well. Am-I-elle."* My given name came to me in a new form, and I experienced my name in a new way. I was the feminine of *I am. Wow!*

Every word everywhere, from street signs to license plates, began to deliver symbols to me as if a great puzzle were revealing itself. Numbers in Divine sequences came to the forefront of my mind (5555, 1313, 1111), and all of this brought forth impeccable presence. What *is* this? I had walked this exact Philadelphia city center street for a year. From Saint Mark's Church to Thirteenth Street, I'd strolled this route every day at the same time, and the circumstances of this day were identical. Yet my inner-freedom experience was revealing something altogether different. To accompany my inner freedom, I let out a laugh so deep, it felt like a deep-tissue massage to my soul body. *Wow!* All the moving parts of the bustling city in perfect harmony synchronized with all the moving parts of the bustling world, which synchronized with all the moving parts of a bustling galaxy and beyond. And little me, one grain of consciousness with the privilege of tapping into all of it for this moment. *Thank you!* Shazam. A new song was being played, a universal rhythm, and I had the ears to hear it: *THAAAAAAAAANK YOUUUUUUUU!*

I had pep in my step. I began to skip. Skip-a-dee-doo-dah. Then I hopped. Hop, hop, hop! *Yay!* Then I started to run. I ran fast, then slowed and jumped a bit. Then I hopped a little more. Again and again and again, all the while twirling about. The energy I was carrying felt dynamic. I was connected to life in a new way. I was alive. I made my way through the city waving, saying hello, and giving high fives to strangers. I spotted a blue Genie boom lift. The Genie lifts were all over the city. The blue booms were used for construction projects. The Genies did the heavy lifting. I'd passed by them hundreds of times walking to and from places in the city but hadn't noticed them as viscerally as I did this day. They were striking.

The hundred-year-old building where I lived (the Chancellor) was in the city center. In Philly, we call it Center City. The Chancellor was such a great location; I was one block from the Walnut Street Theatre and the Wilma Theater. These were home to some of the best musicals and theatrical talent in historic Philadelphia, our nation's first capital. It was so easy to drop into a daytime performance on the fly. The Master of Light meditations I was practicing were seamlessly merging light particles from above into my human experience. The Master of Light meditations were becoming influential in the way that I was experiencing life *tenfold*! So, yes, procuring good theater seats at a great price in meditation happened first, and then I had the pleasure of experiencing what I'd accepted in my mind as reality. These small rewards were a way of appropriating spiritual law that is accessible to all once we accept the responsibility of life and become in alignment with it. We get to do these things for the fun of it! I loved having access to the best vegan restaurants on Society Hill as well. Giggles. I was right where I had always dreamed of being. I was with God.

All of these gorgeous thoughts passed through my consciousness as I strolled home on this particular day. Then the Genie logo on the industrial blue boom lifts jumped out at me suddenly. It had my attention. The scramble of the letters happened. The puzzle was revealed. *Genie. I am-gine.* Giggling to myself, I wondered, *Where did that come from? I am-gine.* And then I saw it: *Imagine.* Imagine means "I *am* a genie." The word broke itself down for me, and it was a miracle. It was here all along, and now I could see it. At that very moment, my understanding and alignment were so surreal. Imagineering had legs. The invisible things were made visible. Through the light, all things took this supportive, illuminating journey. I had only walked some six blocks, and I had seen more in those six blocks than I had as a professional pilot flying around the world. I wanted it to stay, to keep revealing these treasures to me. I became more willing than ever before to stay in the spiritual experience. I love it so much. As I stood there in the center of the city, spiritually taller than I had ever stood before, a greater understanding of one word, "imagination," marked a new epoch of my journey forever.

That afternoon, I was enamored by the interconnected experience I was having with the infinite nature of imagination. Interconnectedness was altogether new. It was being whole in God, as a whole human. Wholeness happened as a direct result of placing my dependence upon my infinite inner resource and allowing it to direct my actions. My directed actions were in accordance with the flow of light codes I was coming to know by way of *direct experience in God.* Dwelling in this state of consciousness allowed for the connection to other things in this miracle of aliveness. The infinite field of *all* possibilities was quite possible. The readily available spiritual experience was the by-product of awakening to the God within myself. I had the space within my consciousness to be one with the *creative intelligence.* Generating the vision of the end result in my mind and feelings came as naturally as the sunrise. The consciousness was a clean canvas when I sat down to meditate; it was miraculous. Clean consciousness was the key to something amazing. Clean consciousness was riches. Creative ideas began flowing into my mind effortlessly. My ideas were stabilized with plans of action. All of it was vivid and full of energy. I colored the ideas onto a physical canvas after meditations. Writing the visions, ideas, and plans of action onto paper mapped out an adventurous journey. There was so much joy in allowing myself this opportunity and having the space and time to complete it. Once the blueprints were in place, I would go further into imagination via the *light portal* and place myself in the center of the drawing. It was essential to imagine from the first person. I was experiencing the entire vision as if I were there, and I *was* there. Since this was the beginning of letting the Master of Light meditation guide me fully, I had many questions. *Was I to continue with the meditation when the manifestation began? Was I to begin manifesting something new at that point?* The *creative intelligence* contin-ued to provide magnificent imagery, so I drew whatever came to mind. I was *in* the drawings. I fell into them effortlessly like falling into a quantum gap.

The co-creating was phenomenal. There were seamless transitions from thought to manifestation, not exactly what I had drawn but like-kind energy. This was the greatest show on Earth. This is what it meant to be alive. The mystery of how God would bring this manifestation was a whole universe in and of itself. Each manifestation package came with all the necessary lessons for me to appropriate the spiritual princi-ples, and it was my duty to continue harnessing my God con-sciousness to bring about the best possible outcome for good and for all.

Ahhhh, I worked for God, and God always wins.

It was time to travel. I packed a small bag, grabbed my stu-dious Moscot black frames, and headed straight for the airport. As I was booking my ticket *on the way* to the airport, my fingers hit a few random buttons on my smartphone, and an incredibly beautiful picture of the aurora borealis (the northern lights) appeared. Stunning prisms of celestial energy in emerald were suspended in abstract art across the night sky. The electri-cally charged particles were dancing above our atmosphere and were synchronistic in rhythm. I remembered a myth once told to me. Aurora borealis are celestial energies preparing to become human. They descend into the Earth plane at a cer-tain time to join the other aspects of the humanoid system (the physical and the spiritual). The celestial energies were the soul bodies, the consciousness bodies. Because of the aurora bore-alis phenomena, couples would travel to the aurora borealis and conceive during this time of year, hoping to attract the celestial energies. This brought innocent peace to me, an inner smile. I didn't fully accept or reject the idea of the myth but was thankful for the pure and playful thoughts entering my consciousness. The free flow of ideas with supernatural beings inspired my journey. Refocusing on the captivating photography on my smartphone, a description read: "October is the best time of year to be here now." It was the optimal time of year to see the northern lights, so Alaska would be my first stop. It dawned on me that I had just discovered where I would be traveling. The connection with Spirit was so rich with inner faith, I was time traveling. I was receiving in a new way. I was outside of thinking, doubting, and planning. I was open-minded. I was allowing. My consciousness was filled with a continuous flow of beautiful things. I was manifesting at the speed of light. All of the elements aligned perfectly—from the heavily discounted airline rate (purchased on the way to the airport) to being upgraded to first class (upon check-in at the gate)! My Alaskan hotel was also practically free, with all the rewards I'd been granted at check-in. With poise, I took my seat on the airliner in my royal-blue beret as a first-class passenger. I usually was the one flying the jet. Now, I was a passenger. I was a personal, intimate friend of the Creator, and I was experiencing greater portions of creation. Every person I encountered smiled at me, was inviting, and was beyond helpful. All the elements of every circumstance had a smile to them. I recognized every detail, even though traveling through time-space continuum in this way inspired new ideas I relate to time. A two-week spiritual experience had started all on its own. As I carried the light, the light continued to carry me. Like those delicate minutes when a child makes her first attempt at riding a horse and finally gets on—and the unruly horse takes off wildly. That was how it was for me. I was holding on to the reins of a power so much greater than myself, and I was in for the ride of my life. *Wheeee!*

Arriving in Alaska gave significant context to the great outdoors. We are talking ginormous wilderness. Alaska wilderness is pure nature. Civilization must accommodate the wild, not the other way around. Feeling the presence of dropping into a *National Geographic* scene is real. Breathing the Alaskan air is like being submerged in an oxygen chamber. The largest organ of my body, my skin, was thanking me by glowing. The air molecules in Alaska are untouched. The air whispers, it is so clean. The air itself detoxifies you, and for the first time, I smelled fresh air. Yes, fresh air has a scent. As I passed through the lobby of the hotel where I had reserved a room, an advertisement caught my eye. It was for a northern lights tour that would be departing from the hotel in the morning at 3:00 a.m. I grabbed the paper and made my reservation for the following morning. I could barely sleep with all the energy passing through my mind and body. Three o'clock in the morning arrived. A mysterious white van pulled up to the hotel valet. It looked as though it had driven through the Alaskan bush to get there. A mystical, heavyset man stepped out from the van. His boots were knee-high suede, slightly covered by wool pants gathered at the tops. Dressed like a caribou hunter, he wore a super-warm-looking brown suede cap that had colored pins on it. The pins resembled the bracelets around his wrists reading *pura vida*, meaning "pure life" in Spanish. I recognized them right away due to their eye-catching array of rainbow colors. The vivid primary colors appealed to all of my senses, making the beginning of this adventure pleasantly sensual. My smile was drenched in humility. The intelligence and potentiality of each particle of this new quantum space was breathtaking. My smile met his eyes, and he smiled back like a grandfather recognizing his long-lost granddaughter. God was in everything. The God in everything was responding to me. His hair was long and gray, evoking wisdom that wrapped gently around his shoulders to meet his beard. He was wearing a copper bracelet on his left wrist, and my eye caught the details. It was engraved with "Aloha." *Wow.* An Alaskan caribou hunter carrying the aloha. "Good morning, dear," he said to me. "I'm your Alaskan chariot up to the northern lights." Dropping into my consciousness was this thought:

All the power that ever was or ever will be is here now.

He came around the back of the van to the side door and opened it. The northern lights were already in full motion; we would begin to catch more of them on our drive up north. I was the only taker of the tour. My inner dialogue chimed in: *Is this safe? Am I safe? Is he safe?* I took a deep breath, absorbed it all, paused, and made the decision. "Well," I said to him, "I've come this far." Then I took a leap of faith and hopped in.

Along the way, he shared stories about the sacred nature of hunting caribou. Being vegan, I was intrigued with his deeply held spiritual beliefs around animal sacrifice. In detail, he talked about the ancient dance and sacrificial ceremony that took place prior to each honest hunt. He was covered in buffalo-like clothing that jingled, and he looked absolutely stoic as he told these stories. His gentle-giant nature came through as he spoke, transporting me into a Siberian-like fairy tale. I complimented him on his aloha mauna . . . And then another synchronicity dawned on me. Hawaiians knew of the hidden manna. *Mauna* was the spirit element to the aloha. The aloha mauna was a way of honoring the light in each and every one of us. This was embedded in Hawaiian culture all along. I love seeing examples of God's law being universally accepted across diverse cultures. Aloha was an example of a new way to experience God's law in Hawaiian culture. Thank God my eyes could see. The guide said his daughter was responsible for his aloha bracelet. He told the story of a daughter he very much admired. She had moved to Hawaii years before to practice the spirit of aloha, *the light within.* He continued to acknowledge her respect for all of nature. The One was telling me a story (through the experience of others) about the world, one human and one experience at a time. Thank God my ears could hear.

The planetary space over us began to illuminate. The aurora borealis was in full motion and drew closer and closer as we drove farther north. The air itself was alive, and I could feel beast-size wildlife near. *All is well. All is well.* We arrived at a beautiful lodge in the forest where a beautiful cottage awaited me. The first indications of the sun rising were when the natural night-lights that coursed the sky began to fade. The promise of a new day was beginning. The day would begin here in the presence of northern lights travelers. Everything and everyone was new. The northern lights travelers were from around the world, and I was able to procure new information from each one of them. This was the way I learned best. Traveling, exploring, discovering with a direct experience with God. The sunlight came and went faster than ever, and the birth of the night-lights was visible and in full dance across the sky. We would receive a splendid illustration of the dancing light energy once again.

The next day, I departed from the lodge to find the Chena Hot Springs and the magical World War II airplane site, which was parked in the middle of a snowy forest. The steam of the hot springs was easy to spot. I decided to stay there for a few nights to rejuvenate and finally sleep. White puffy snow lay out in a panorama, as if I were living in my own enchanted snow globe. The hot springs were nestled perfectly amid the amazing Douglas firs, drooping with white.

Morning meditation was the most sacred time of the day. Specifically, between the hours of 4:00 to 6:00 a.m. was *Divine* time. This is the time the angels were taking their orders and giving them too. This was the optimal time to align with the Master of Light meditation. Morning in the Chena Hot Springs arrived, and *I let myself go,* now in the water. I dipped into my imagination as I dipped into the steaming fluidity. Once submerged in the light portal, I became a mermaid. Swimming eloquently with whale sharks in a phytoplankton-rich sea. I dove deeper into God consciousness and began discovering octopuses along the seafloor. My long, wavy hair flowed weightless in the support of the sea's *pikai*. Pikai is a traditional Hawaiian ceremony where seawater is used to purify harmful energies from a person. The seawater was alive, and like nature, it knew how to nourish and purify my mermaid hair effortlessly. This cleansing of my hair was symbolic of the deep dive into God consciousness. Fully submerged in God consciousness now, I began to observe the breathless emotions and the *need* for air. Allowing the *need* to pass, still very deep in my imagination, the magnificent Mauna Loa volcano erupted right in front of me. Her purging sent sound waves through the underwater colonies, bringing awareness to just another one of nature's gripping phenomena. The strength of the pikai was revealed once more as the scarlet-orange lava dripped into the sea like a lava lamp. Highly organized underwater colonies accepted my presence. Adherence to the underwater flow was mandatory. Obedience to Mother Nature was not optional here. I swam among the sea life in awe.

Immersed in aqua-colored water, like in a passing dream, a ruby-red helicopter caught my eye above the sea. I focused on it until *I was flying it* over the rich chocolate lava of the Big Island of Hawaii. I flew in front of the waterfalls, and as I got closer to them, I could *feel* their energy of letting go being communicated through the waterfalls. Everything was a sign. Through this feeling of unspeakable freedom, I took in every imaginable drop of water as it flowed down the mountainous rock. Each particle within the liquid carried a great message of natural wonders. The frequency of sound produced by the synchronized helicopter rotors, accompanied by the wind, resonated deeply within my DNA.

I was in the *how* of a quantum jump. I had claimed the *what*. I had persisted in the pineal gland meditation, day by day, night by night, and voilà! I was experiencing the perfect unfolding of events from the infinite intelligence. Like an incredible whale breach in all of its destined magnificence, from the Alaskan hot springs, my dreams had emerged, and I was in the *belly of the whale!* I faced north and bowed; I faced east and bowed; I faced south and bowed; I faced west and bowed. "Thank you." Nobility and honor settled into my awareness. Quantum intelligence was coloring inside the lines of my imagination. I had no idea *how* wonderful life could be. This was my firsthand experience of opening the door to new fields of vast exploration. The quantum field of all possibilities was at hand. This magnificent quantum intelligence transported me to the big, beautiful island of Kona, Hawaii.

The next stop was the Garden of the Gods in Colorado. More about the centermost point of my mind, the pineal gland, would be revealed here. I sat in the Garden of the Gods for sunrise and sunset while sun-gazing for several days. Sun-gazing was a way to electrically charge the centermost point of my mind, the mind's eye. I was drawn to this place and this practice; at the time, I had no research on the efficacy of the sun-gazing exercise. This was happening in the quantum leap. I was being led to do these things. The Master of Light meditation unfolded organically. I both found and developed it through the practice of meditation. I sought it. In a natural way, I went right to the centermost point of my mind in meditation. In doing so, my forehead began to tingle like it was turning on. As I persisted in the observation on the centermost point of my mind, more parts of my physical body began to first illuminate, then awaken. The awakening felt alive, healthy, and joyful. I journaled about the new information arriving in my consciousness, as I would practice this for hours. "Awakened" meant my soul body, spirit body, and physical body were in alignment. This alignment rendered my mind, thoughts, and feelings as an interconnected *Divine* order. I was firing on all cylinders with solution-based ideas; world-peace ideas. All elements of the quantum leap were personally tailored to the God consciousness I was carrying. *It* knew everything that was needed and appeared to have a sense of humor too.

New ways to pray were revealed during the quantum leap. These higher-nature light codes were governing my being. Praying was attractive and empowering. All kinds of goodness were flowing into my life. Now I had the power to pray!

Forms of Prayer

1. Drawing out our good from the universe with the spoken word.
2. Scientific prayer in the form of gratitude in written form.
3. Positive attitude.
4. Kneeling to the Father in secret.
5. Singing and dancing.
6. The art of blessing and praising.

There are no shortcuts in the spiritual experience. I trusted that my intention, followed by my action, would manifest a new experience where I would learn and grow. This was *faith in action.* By the time awareness of *I am* arrived, I had applied all of the previous knowledge and shown sufficient faith to proceed successfully. The *I am* application from a sober state pole-vaulted me to an apex of understanding the wisdom of *I am* from my current state of consciousness. Keeping my question simple—*Who am I?*—was enough. The beauty of the answers is that they continued to build upon themselves. It was marvelous. The fulfillment of love produced completeness. My faith foundation was a firm bedrock upon which all good things would be built within a truly sustainable ecosystem. My original nature was here, and my gifts and talents were beginning to activate. The new intelligence I needed was being downloaded.

My sense of duty rose with all the power necessary to carry out the responsibility of life and my individual life contract. The efficacy of my work was interlacing with the consciousness I was carrying, along with its ability to interact with the spiritual principles that governed human existence. Similar to practicing man-made laws and them becoming second nature. I had the strong desire to practice spiritual principles until they were instinctive. Drawing out our good from the universe by speaking our desires into midair is a beatitude. Beatitudes translate as "supreme blessedness." When I affirm out loud my well-being, *I am well*, in the present moment. I'm literally drawing out my good from the invisible and making it an actual fact. The right alignment of my consciousness (aligning my will with the will of God) is essential in regard to the tangible results manifested (*what I will see*). I have inner faith in the power of my God consciousness, and I accept my proclamation as a known fact. I therefore move into acceptance of the "done deal" through acts of wellness. In this way, I draw further wellness into my presence. The practice of this beatitude is then considered to be *right action*.

Through "scientific" prayer, I exercise inner faith in written form. "Science" is from the Latin word meaning knowledge. I may be experiencing an ailment in some part of my body, so I write: "I am grateful for my health." I focus on the parts of me that are healthy. This is a solution-based idea. I am working with the unseen to bring forth my *new idea* of health. In written prayer, *I am* turning my body to light. The mysterious *I am* is unchangeable. *I am* is within each and every one of us and will never be forgotten. *I am* begets *I am*. The awareness of *I am* is a spiritual awakening in and of itself. I may forget *who I am, what I am,* or *where I am*—but I can never forget that *I am.* Once we write it, we accept it, and can thus wield it. *I am* is an illumination.

Our positive attitude in any situation brands our faith. When we are sure of the working of the unseen, we feel joy. We are no longer on our own power; we have the power of our will in alignment with God's will, and thus our application of spiritual principles is in the light. Our trust mirrors steadfastness. Our hearts smile, because we *know* good things are coming and that all is well. Seeking a greater consciousness was one part of the whole. Applying what I found was the second part. Applying what I found in full alignment—that was the competence part. And taking responsibility for the tangible results of my manifestations—that is what it means to be spiritually awake. Spiritual awakenings happen as we have the capacity to take greater responsibility. Intimacy ("in-to-me-see") is the ability to go within and sustain the relationship with God. The aligning of my consciousness with God's consciousness manifests revelations; these revelations are our clear-cut directions. They are perfectly clear.

Prior to the psychic change, kneeling to pray was what religious people did in church. I respected this method, but I wasn't captivated by *kneeling to my Father in secret* until this method entered my own consciousness *on its own* in the form of a new idea. All of a sudden, the idea was attractive, the direct experience with God was attractive. My awareness was intrigued by the unseen. When I actually tried it, and *kneeled to my Father in secret,* my prayers would be answered, one by one. Traveling on "my own power" was nil in comparison to turning my will over to God. On my own power, my thinking was arrogant. It thought I was responsible for the good in my life. I wasn't consciously arrogant, nor did I think the idea that I was responsible for the good in my life was arrogant, but a closer look at my attitudes revealed I *did* think I was responsible for the good in my life. Prayer was the sacred gateway where I would speak to God. It was only in *full* surrender of "my own power" to the will of God, that level of humility that *requires* wholehearted *humbleness*, that the flow of God began to happen for yours truly.

Returning to the Center City of Philadelphia after this enlightening two-week spiritual experience led me to believe it was time to settle my affairs there. I hadn't any precise ideas at the forefront of my consciousness, but I began to follow suit anyway. Beginning to understand co-creating allowed me to take on more responsibility, placing my trust where it belonged: on the Creator of All Things.

Service to others would be my swag. Whatever I could do to help. The continual cleansing of the consciousness turned over its leaf to usefulness. Small acts of kindness like holding the door open for others multiplied themselves. Other generous acts like taking others through the twelve steps of recovery multiplied good in all channels. Taking time to listen to people and their stories multiplied healings. The service wheel gained momentum, and with its momentum I received a call from the private jet company that managed the jet I flew. I had served two years as lead captain, overseeing all elements of the jet business while flying around the world. Our off time was when the jet wasn't flying after my on-ground flight duties were complete. That actually meant quite a bit of time off, but I was still on call nonetheless. The expectation of the operation was that we could launch within twenty-four hours from the call. Once we were notified, we had twenty minutes to respond. This was the understanding, and it was adhered to in every way. Flying is a lifestyle. Flying is a detail-oriented, precise exercise where everything must go absolutely right the first time every time. It is a process of staying on your toes, and the elements surrounding the event hold the same attention to detail.

Over the phone, the aircraft management company informed me the jet would be down for extensive maintenance over the next few weeks. They proceeded to tell me that this would be a paid vacation for me, and I could go anywhere I chose during this time. I could travel. My heart burst; this was the first time in ten years that I'd ever heard of such a thing. A five-week vacation! OMG. Vacations were things other people did. I usually was the pilot taking others on their vacations. Now it was my turn to have my very own vacation. Since I'd begun my professional flying career, I'd spent every holiday—every single one—on the flight deck or away from home flying others around on their vacations and business affairs. I'd been shadowing the life of millionaires, seeing the world through their eyes. Eighty percent of the flights I piloted I'd categorized as stunning adventures. Now, could it really be my turn? The voice on the other end of the line said, "Don't swallow your tongue, Amielle." They knew the kind of magic they were delivering to me was super special for a jet jockey.

"Yes! Yes!" I sang. "Thank you, thank you!" I could hear the music, and I was dancing. Interestingly, I immediately began planning my trip to Hawaii, the Big Island. Could it be? Could the quantum field be presenting the deep dive into God consciousness I had experienced while in the Alaskan hot springs? Full of wonder, bliss was a sign. The manifestation was coincidental, to say the least. Out of nothingness . . . came something. This proved it. I chose to believe this was all God. It was working. I danced all throughout my high-rise apartment with gratitude. This hundred-year-old building had made more history. My joy was stored in its walls; it would be there forever. I had so much to be grateful for! Hip, hip, hooray! With a keen awareness of the spoken word, and my ability to surrender internal dialogues at once while depending upon God for every detail of every matter, I kept my focus where it belonged: on my God duties. I flourished living within my own sustainable, internal government, driven by an all-inclusive love. The positive responsiveness from outside of me was an additional asset to the individualization of my inner freedom. *I am co-creating! Do-da! Do-da!*

After the psychic change, being connected to God, my soul mate, was as powerful as experiencing the successes of others as if they were my own. This was so different from having the fear of missing out. The sense of accomplishment others were receiving from their *direct experience with God* was shared. Equally important, I had the power to cry and grieve with others too. I never needed to change people or outside events to be okay. In some instances, I could empathize and, in others, sympathize. I had the power to accept others as they were in the moment, not needing to change them. If an undesirable or despised state of suffering appeared, I'd bless it and praise it. I'd give it my full blessing. If a perceived setback appeared, I'd give it my full blessing. I'd bless it and praise it right out of existence. I'd give my blessings and praise to the good stuff too! Not only did this understanding of how to give circumstances my blessing further sustain my alignment with the spiritual principles—it kept me inside of God consciousness. I was a long way from the victimhood state of consciousness, in which there was no access to the miracle of life. I had passed Go, I had collected *my soul*, and I had won the *cosmic lotto*.

A MYSTERIOUS BUBBLE RIGHT IN FRONT OF MY FACE

The final days in Philadelphia were here. I was on my way home from a local yoga studio in an area known as Fishtown. Omnipotent presence was all mine. My state of being was the best I had ever known and beyond what I could have ever wished possible. Morning yoga was a way of aligning mind, body, and spirit. The ancient asana practice was the predecessor to all forms of martial arts. A daily yoga practice demanded reverence in acceptance of oneself—in *the now*. In my acceptance, I had the absolute awareness that *all is well*. "Absolute" meant if I was having an experience that *all is not well*, then I undoubtedly knew self-will (ego) had gotten in between my God consciousness and me. Instinctively, self-discipline activated, and I would turn over the lower natures of the ego (attachments and the rejection of my inner God consciousness) to the One Who Has All Power and All Knowledge. God. Through this, I was learning a new way to love: a love that allowed for others to be free; a love that allowed others to think, act, and follow their inclinations; and a love that allowed others to follow their soul's choice and make decisions based on their own beliefs. God was the soul mate of each individual, and all souls were accounted for by God.

I had overheard in yoga circles while in Europe people talking about the spiritual principle of fasting. The love I was carrying had opened my eyes to all beings. My opinions about people had vanished. I could see people and hear people like never before. This was fascinating. Common themes would come through the people I was visiting, and I would be aware of the common themes people were delivering. That was the most beautiful part of God being every individual's soul mate. The taxi driver, the housekeeper, the bellboy, *et al* could be the most enlightened soul. You never knew how God was going to use people *for the good of all*. That was also the beauty of full reliance on God. I gained access to all of God's people *for the good of all*. Soul bodies align in the grace of God. This was part of the mystical phenomena of trusting God with all of the details of conscious manifestation. Even in a space filled with conversation, or a traffic jam on the freeway, God's message would find me, and it was always there.

Fasting was new to me. I began by refraining from food starting at 6:00 p.m. and into the next day until noon after yoga practice. This opened up more space to meditate and journal. Journaling had become a way of life. It was letters and notes to God. Pen to paper was how I practiced gratitude to God. Journaling was a form of prayer. I made all my requests to God in my journal. I kept track of recurring dreams as well. Journaling was a gateway to God. When I felt stable with an eighteen-hour fasting period, I would further lighten my intake of food during the remaining six hours. At times, I would consume only wheatgrass juice and water until 2:00 p.m. This left four hours in a twenty-four-hour period for nutrients. I became highly conscious of elements that brought forth maximum benefits in the smallest quantities. I treated it like an adventure.

The rhythm of my fast was carried by my intention to grow closer to God. I was learning the power of intention through this simple process. I found it was getting easier to reach deeper states of meditation while I was fasting. With my flexibility increasing in the physical yoga class, new revelations with God opened my body. The practice of holding yoga entanglements and binds for long periods while directing the spirit body, the breath of life, allowed for further dissipation of attachments, which opened my mind to further knowledge. This overall openness would advance my service to others, creating a real-world impact. Yoga was a science of service for *the good of all*. The consciousness called for spiritual cleansing first, then Spirit led my body into periodic fasting. Overall cleanliness was desirable. In the apex of fasting, greater space and capacity for more love consciousness flowed into my internal government. Holding postures for longer periods of time with minimal food in the body enabled a clear pathway to direct the spirit body, the breath of life, into the crevices of the physical body that needed it most. The longer I was in a pose, the more I could heal an area of the body. Taking my time through eloquent transitions, not wanting to miss one piece of this great puzzle that was revealing itself to me, I felt reborn in new and beautiful ways. Yoga was about slowing everything down: slow was smooth, and smooth was fast.

So there I was on my way home, carrying my inner-freedom state, committed to my fasting experience. My senses were fully alive, and the air carried the whistles of the universe as I brought my car to a stop at the red light. I had a Tibetan singing bowl beat playing at a low decibel. The car came to a full stop, and I ever so slightly leaned my head forward. Not a conscious movement but rather an inadvertent tilt forward. My forehead pressed up against an invisible balloon right in front of my face, and then my entire head went inside of the balloon. Nothingness. This bubble was the furthest, longest, widest infinity and went on *forever*. I became what was inside of it. I was one with it. Infinity. Eternity. Forevermore.

The entire experience lasted seconds. My mind grasped at nothingness. It could not fathom what had just happened. The greatest experience of my life was unexplainable nothingness. When I took my first breath, the bubble was gone. My head moved ever so slightly, and it was gone. *Whoa!* I looked at the traffic light as it turned green. I proceeded forward into normal life. I was completely fascinated. I tried to move my head forward the rest of the way home—but nothing. What was that? Where had I slipped into? My God, it goes on forever. It was inconceivably out of this world! I had entered into a dimension that existed right in front of my face. A miraculous dimension invisible to the naked eye that propelled the onset of spiritual experience with higher intelligences in greater portions of creation. Here I was, a little human having these profound spiritual experiences beyond my wildest dreams. I called the only friend at the time I felt I could share this new dimension with, but they couldn't hear me. They didn't understand. I told the story again, slowing down again to explain every detail—but they still couldn't hear me.

Attempting to describe nothingness was my dilemma. Unwavering, my mind reflected on how people would ask me a question about a specific situation, and I would reference the nature of God's law, yet their consciousness couldn't receive the revelation yet. Love and tolerance for others flowed into my consciousness. All I had was love. Agape love. Wicked how we can only hear at our own level of consciousness. Better yet, we can only hear at the cleanliness of the consciousness we carry. The depths we have met ourselves allow for crystal-clear communication with God. Full dissolution of the ego is required.

THE MODERN MYSTERY SCHOOL

God's *how* had arrived. I landed on the big, beautiful island of Kona, Hawaii. I was learning to fly helicopters as well as being introduced to free diving. It was a new chapter of my life—a quantum jump! Amazing how the act of skydiving had matured into quantum jumping. Had God been preparing me all along? My personally tailored life by God. In the middle of the Pacific Ocean and in between a chain of islands, I was learning how to combine air and movement with water and purity. I brought five thousand hours of airplane brain into this newness. I was now being taught to see aerodynamics with new eyes. I was being taught the dynamics of flow, the breathtaking connection between fluidity and form. The vivid teal waters with gigantic waves rising up symbolized the potentiality of energy. Then the waves would bend into the perfect circular pattern of the golden ratio every time. It was so beautiful. Every water molecule and all of the wave's energy was accounted for as it rinsed the lava beaches before returning to the depths, from spaces both wild and organized. Seamless mind and energy were awaiting wave potentiality once more by the mind's eye.

The power that could bring observation into full potential-ity was the alignment of human will with God's will. Full atten-tion on all the details of every moment. To stay present with our God consciousness and to keep our God consciousness in front, above, and underneath preconceived ideas; remember-ing every idea before this moment is a preconceived idea. Our responsibility is to gather it in mind, then patiently await the discovery of it. There it was, in its full expression: nature giving us a show as I learned to hover the helicopter with a beginner's mind. The largest active volcano on the planet, Mauna Loa, which rises to a height of 13,600 feet, was active. The energy of her magma was the promise of a psychic change, a shift in elements of science until her energy surpassed the exchange and brought a full-on eruption: quantum access. Viewing the eruption from the Robinson helicopter was a surreal illustra-tion of birth, life, and death, with its heat, color, and resilience adding to the ambiance of our joy flight.

"My cup runneth over" (Psalms 23.5). Hawaii flying was captivating with full-moon flights to waterfalls and black-sand beaches. Free diving was a way to explore highly organized, under-the-sea colonies. Free diving was the sustainable solu-tion for keeping our core temperatures cool throughout the microclimate of arid and hot (the Big Island has eight microcli-mates). At the end of adventurous days, turning on my Balinese lamp to prepare for the nightly ritual of gratitude was instinc-tive. I glanced at the detail of the bamboo bed. The estate I was blessed to accommodate was fully furnished with Balinese furniture and accessories, all possible by the grace of God. The Indonesian decor added to the mystical atmospheres of the magical island. I had an appreciation for the handmade furni-ture and the spirit it carried from a faraway land. The geckos seemed to love it too. They were lime green and communi-cated often in chiming tones. They knew right when to affirm a thought I was having with their vocalized chirps. I loved having them around. Veganism allows for full connection with all beings; especially animals. The idea of eating an animal becomes unbearable because you begin to respect them and their right to life, like you respect humans' right to life. This was a natural purification process as animals' consciousness departs the cells of my body. *You are what you eat.* That actually proved to be true! The property was home to hundreds of palm trees with thousands of baby coconuts. Each morning I would take the ladder to a palm tree of my liking and climb up to reach the sweet fruits of the tree. There I was in the future of my imagination in living color.

The single-street village where God placed me was Puako. Puako was known by Hawaiians to have one of the most resourceful and resilient ecosystems in all of Hawaii. The Hawaiian heart was smiling upon my presence. I had entered the aloha in ways I didn't even know were possible. You see, the Big Island of Hawaii has eight of the thirteen climates of the world. This amounts to big energy readily available to anyone who will receive it. From the nightstand, I pulled out my journal, opened it, and something I wrote on the top of one of the pages caught my eye. It read: "The Modern Mystery School." A traveler in passing had mentioned it to me as I departed the East Coast for Hawaii. Remembering the name, the Modern Mystery School, it caught my attention indeed. I had nonchalantly jotted it down. I had never heard of a mystery school. What is it? These were questions for the Master of Light meditation. It had been weeks before, and now it was jumping off the paper: *here I am, here I am.* Miracles were the new normal, though, and I easily accepted them. I would only stay in Hawaii for four months before returning to the mainland. Only, this time, I would return to the West Coast, to my California home.

The first call to the Modern Mystery School (MMS) was a beckoning for me to answer the call from quantum intelligence. This was Thy idea for Thy serving. Daily, in morning meditation, I was asking God, *How can I best serve Thee?* My attention was drawn to the top of the page of my journal, which read, "The Modern Mystery School." I was learning to receive. After all, whatever is asked is given. The Modern Mystery School was the new invisible door in front of me. The willingness to serve God was the golden key. Only God opens doors. The door was open; my part was to walk through it. The initiation into advanced spiritual training began with a galactic initiation. This is the process of becoming a galactic human. Galactic humans have access to other intelligent and energetic forms in our galaxy. Both the initiation and the activation brought forth an abundance of light-energy mind awareness with further clarity of *who I am, what I am, where I am from,* and *what I am doing* here on the Earth plane. I was introduced to the Hierarchy of Light. Humbling. Through the teachings and practices of the rituals taught at MMS, individual people's lives were illustrations of exponential spiritual, mental, and emotional human growth. Never before experienced, but my humanoid system loved it. The responsiveness I received from the universe after practicing the rituals made it clear. Immersion into the *brotherhood and sisterhood of light* profoundly assisted my courage and strength and compelled me to get on with serving my Divine life contract. The new spiritual rituals and trainings felt silly at first, yet the tangible results weren't silly at all. The guidance from the Hierarchy of Light was useful tenfold, and I liked having an army of light above and all around me. We are not alone. The more I practiced the rituals, more rituals were revealed. I had developed a spiritual tool kit for Earth. All spiritual discoveries continued to build upon themselves in sustainable ways. It became evident that the Modern Mystery School was an advanced spiritual training that appeared so that I could find my spiritual family here on the Earth plane. My human path merged with my galactic path.

As a way of manifesting consciously, I began practicing alchemy meditation. In the alchemical process, I used sacred geometry (geometric shapes) with solfeggio frequencies (174 hertz, 285 hertz, 396 hertz, 417 hertz, 528 hertz, 639 hertz, 741 hertz) to bring an idea into full fruition. This alchemical process supported going deeper and staying longer in God consciousness during a meditative state. It also became a medium for the transmutation of negative energies into positive ones—as well as a transformation of an idea into full fruition. With a clean canvas ready for new manifestations, I began the journey of toning while in deep states of God consciousness. I also practiced imagineering (the act of visualization while connected to our inner portal of light) while in deep meditation. Having zero expectations of the *how* was essential. When I found myself trying to control the outcome of any particular manifestation either consciously or subconsciously, I would resurrender to God's will by turning it over to the "Father of lights" (James 1:17) who presided over me. In simple terms: *I'd admit complete defeat AND ask for God's help in the matter at hand.* This would dissolve any residual ego in between the work of God and my God consciousness. With these ancient meditation techniques, ideas began arriving in physical form (tangible results) in sustainable ways. This process was a gem. Like a new scientist, I did my very best to apply the alchemy meditation with a sincere heart and great reverence. The new ideas continued arriving in physical form.

The ancient teachings of MMS have been protected for thousands of years. Our lineage in the Modern Mystery School International is the third order of King Salomon. The teachings have been kept intact by handing them down from the guide's mouth to the initiate's ear. Accepting *God willing* was a considerable responsibility. It was the joining of my will with the will of God while harnessing my light-energy mind with newfound power. This involved a collaborative process of letting go and embracing the spiritual experience as it unfolded before me. In this, there was to be no clinging to results. The results far more belonged to God. I was just a trusted servant of them.

Ownership of things meant attachment and entrapment. Being a trusted servant allowed enjoying them, and meant knowing with absolute certainty that I was responsible for what I would see. It was all within. The advanced spiritual training added greater sustenance to my intention of service. With so much beauty coming through on this level of ascension, my humble question continued day in and day out: *How can I best serve Thee?* The mission of the Modern Mystery School is Shamballah: peace on Earth.

Becoming a galactic human required spiritual instincts. It was seeking God in everything. It was seeking to understand God through direct experience. The rituals were all about direct experiences with God, and they worked. The more I could get out of my own way, the more I could experience God in everything. Less me, more we. I practiced meditations ritually. Meditation is an exercise of faith. Meditation's serenity led me to a local internet cafe one afternoon. The cafe was moderately busy with people coming and going. It was the perfect atmosphere for me to blend in while I gave forty-five minutes to drawing closer to God. I put my sunglasses on, opened my computer, and placed my hands over the keys as if I were typing. I looked like Ray Charles with my dark oval-shaped frames and hands perched on the keyboard. The cultivation of music was from within while tapping my inner faith (the unseen light particles). Its rhythm aligned me with the greatest show on Earth. I began to meditate by focusing my eyes on the space in between objects. Once I captured the space, I would expand it. I would then focus on the space between me and the objects. Again, I would expand that space, like *falling* into it. Like removing layers of the invisible veil—harnessing my will while in alignment with the will of God. Finally, my focused sharpened on the space right in front of my face and then, once again, expanded it. I was in. The technique is similar to a 3D art image with a secret picture inside it. When you focus on the image long enough and let your eyes go, a picture appears as you proclaim, "I see it!" Only, in this exercise, I was focusing on midair and finding the air within the air as a way of expanding space. The meditation then guided me to lean into the space in between air. Not thinking anything of it, I leaned into it and—abracadabra! There I was again, in *the gap* inside the balloon of nothingness. Blip. My consciousness merged with *the gap,* and it expanded beyond what could be conceived. It was *gigantic!* G.I.N.O.R.M.O.U.S. The space of nothingness carried me like an octopus with legs and arms in a forever position. Wiggly. Its reach was *infinite.* Beyond. I was experiencing infinite. *I am infinite.* I had a thought, and *blip,* it disappeared. *Whoa!* Another quantum leap. I was so elated that I'd found the bubble that I started singing "zip-a-dee-doo-dah" again! An audience of people began to laugh throughout the cafe at my childlike joy. A single thought removed me from *the gap.* There was a download from the One that was happening while within *the gap.*

I grabbed my smartphone, found the contact for the guide of the meditation, and shouted with glee, "I entered *the gap!*" Eight months earlier, in my car, I'd entered *the gap* for the first time. I didn't even know that's what the mysterious bubble was called. I had no idea I would learn about *the gap* from her meditation. I didn't have any expectations of *the gap.* "I'm so grateful. Thank you," I said.

There was silence. I hadn't been able to tell anyone of this phenomenon; they couldn't *hear* me. But now someone knew precisely what I was talking about and had made a guided meditation to assist people in entering *the gap.* She answered with great humility and neither confirmed nor denied what I was saying. She simply said, "Keep trying."

That was enough work for the day. This was positive confirmation that my spiritual family was with me. Practicing meditation was the way. I had found others with like-kind passion for higher consciousness. What I was seeking was also seeking me. I would continue my spiritual path through the Modern Mystery School. After *the gap* experiences, the imagination exploded, and "beyond good" was the new normal. I was brand-new to attempting world peace with conscious manifestation—or was I? Hadn't I been trying to balance my inner peace all along? Inspired by the loving consciousness of the mysteries, I gladly accepted the position of a "light worker" manifesting world peace. This wasn't an advertisement, however; it was an inner knowing of what needs to be done and doing it. All work on the altruistic plane, once complete, was forgotten, and that is what allows it to be carried into the eternal. Doing for others without being found out was the exercise. I could reach more people this way. I thought about how many others were here, and when our paths would cross here on the Earth plane. The nurturing of God filled every cell of my body. I was home.

CHAPTER 5

THE SPIRITUAL PRINCIPLE OF I AM

Who am I?

The idea of linear time was uprooted after the psychic change. A foundation of trusting the process was developed. The God infrastructure within my internal government was reinforced by an ever-expanding daily meditation practice. Boundless time superseded using time as a weapon toward myself and others. All limiting beliefs around time fell away. I went from inner dialogues of never having enough time and missing out on things I loved because I held myself to an age-appropriate timeline, to freedom from the suffering of using time as a means to an end. Time became charming. Time became moments of treasure. There was only Divine time, and I relied on it.

These revelations of time built upon themselves as new ideas in my mind by living the "prayer of asking" in meditation.

The prayer of asking allowed me to have a direct connection to God where all things would be revealed. If I had a question, God had an answer. I asked, *How old am I?* My age was: *human becoming galactic.* I was from eternity, and I would return to eternity. Becoming a human was a blip, then galactic human, then I don't know. I was in an infinite evolutionary journey, and time was empowering. A stronger foundation of faith had manifested within my internal government as my connection sustained itself. I spent so much time working on my internal government so that I would instinctively apply spiritual law. My spirit body was kept alive with the breath of life. Spirit and life were at hand. I fully trusted in the unseen—a total reliance upon God, my soul mate. Gratitude fulfilled my entire being as I became immersed in building a *trust fund* rooted in faith. Faith in God's direction contingent upon my willingness to appropriate spiritual law. Wasn't this the root of all trust funds? Wasn't this the original thought of the great minds of our Founding Fathers when they captured the idea of a trust fund? The true meaning of "In God We Trust." Our trust funds would manifest appropriate to our understanding of the quantum field of infinite possibilities. There were cycles of growth defined by the ascension process. *Who am I in time?* Be it now. Past and future were the psychology of organization. Time was now.

In the Master of Light meditation, I continued laying my prayers of asking at the altar of the light within my mind. *Who am I?* I would ask this same question over and over again. *Who am I?* The answers began to grow deeper and deeper. First, my answers were of the world (more physical). Then my answers were derived from the Hierarchy of Light (more esoteric). What was revealed continued to build upon itself. It was a new, sustainable way to explore, discover, and co-create with spirit stuff. Having access to the seat of my soul, the light within my mind was both a privilege and a luxury. A greater understanding of the prayers of asking happened the more I asked it questions. It connected me to *how life works*. There was nothing that I couldn't ask for from God. If it was on my heart to ask, then God placed it there. God came before the thought, and it was my Divine right to seek solutions and to use the prayer of asking. In other words, it was impossible for me to ask for something that didn't already exist, wasn't already given to me. God was not my idea; I AM the idea of God. Understanding *who I am* gave way to the prayer of asking. It was the easier, softer way of receiving. While meditating on my inner light, my forehead would tingle. Giving my full attention to it illuminated my being. I was learning a new way of receiving infinite knowledge through this light portal that was opening within myself. I was learning to communicate with *the unseen*. I was in the business of mastering my inner light, and my desires, my aspirations, and my dreams had been placed on my heart by God. Wow, it was my duty to claim prayer. God awaited my prayers of asking in the spiritual awakening, and it was given.

THE PRESENCE OF LIGHT ENERGY

After a lifetime of seeking higher consciousness, I was beginning to reap what I had sown. Life activation opened the door to new Divine space in the healing world. Life activation was precisely how I would have described every soul decision I had ever made prior to arriving in this state of consciousness. My life was so neat, and life activation described it perfectly. Like picking your favorite ice-cream flavor, I chose the charming kind of life activation. Light was a mode of healing, cleansing, and purifying the consciousness. Both light and consciousness were at the center of the life activation healing modality. I believed in light. Light was the major factor in determining the operation and biological composition of our human systems.

Just watch how the planet comes alive when the sun rises. Take a look at our ocean environments when the sun ignites photosynthesis within them. Our biological makeup is 70 percent water. When light enters into our DNA molecules, the molecules are replenished. Life activation replenishes light in a sequence of three nucleotides, which together form a unit of genetic code in our DNA. It sheds light on our genetic code. Molecules are made up of atoms. Atoms consist of protons, neutrons, and electrons. Protons have a positive charge (i.e., light energy), neutrons have a neutral charge (i.e., light energy), and electrons are fundamental particles with a negative charge (i.e., light energy).

The electron is to the molecule as gravity is to Earth. With the earth comes gravity, and with the molecule comes the electron. Light energy has wave potentiality. We are gaining access to the highest potentiality of our genetic makeup in our life activation by sending light from the celestial into the genetic code. In addition to being here physically on the Earth plane, we are connected through spheres of energy on higher planes of consciousness above us. We have potentiality through *the observation effect* to harness an abundant amount of light energy, as well as to cultivate sustainable structures through the alignment of our will with God's will. For instance, when I began to observe the light in the center of my mind, my observations of it amplified its light, which then magnetized like-kind light. Light magnifies light.

In the alignment of our will with God's will, we gain access to the intelligence of light. This is called the Hierarchy of Light. The Hierarchy of Light includes high-vibrational energies with power beyond human capacity. The Hierarchy of Light upholds the Law of Good. In essence, these high-vibrational energies are light workers. The Law of Good embodies the spiritual principles that govern our existence. When we arrive in a state of consciousness that has access to the Hierarchy of Light, the question is always: *How can I best serve Thee?* These spheres of energy, which allow us to connect to the greater forces of good, carry higher work within them. We are trusted with greater responsibility. Our trust funds grow. These very real spheres of energy are a blueprint for mastering our light, thereby mastering our life.

Identical to sacred geometric patterns, the spheres in patterns live on me, above me, and all around me, repeating themselves eternally. As the genetic code of my DNA is activated through life activation, these spheres light up from the feet to the pelvis, and from the pelvis to the right hip. Then from the right hip to the left hip, the spheres continue up the body, mapping out as a geometric prism. Once the awareness of the spheres becomes available, you have been given the blueprint of life. The natural next step is to pick up the spiritual tools at your feet and use them.

The geometric prism encompasses the whole body and is known as the tree of life. The "tree of life" is an indescribable spiritual ascension here on the Earth plane. Our devotion to the tree of life ascension constitutes altruistic work; those actions done in Spirit we absolutely get to take with us into eternal life. Every opportunity to overcome the negative ego (the lower nature of self, self-centeredness) is afforded, further opening invisible doors. Discernment is cultivated. Greater responsibility is given. In order to uphold the Law of Good, we must be the host of our godliness. The acceptance of our alignment with the will of God is acceptance of our divinity and, essentially, what it means to become a human being. The Hierarchy of Light exists as dimensions of angels, archangels, masters of light, and other light beings with extraordinary capabilities. With conscious awareness of the spheres, we get to collaborate with the Hierarchy of Light. We get to serve the Hierarchy of Light. Our service is in assisting others to understand their godliness. This opportunity is the greatest experience of the human.

The Hierarchy of Light has the tremendous ability to wield love and healings and does so for the evolution of humanity. The activated light within us can call upon celestial light, new light outside the Earth plane, and that which radiates in the Hierarchy of Light. This light is very different from a recycled light within the Earth plane. The astral plane is within the vibratory, heavenly realm of the Hierarchy of Light. On the astral plane, we exist in the opposite sex from what we are here on the Earth plane. Not physical sex, like male or female as we know it to be here on the physical plane of Earth—but male representing expansion and force, female representing contraction and form.

As the sun rises for us each day, we wake up and energetically pull from our astral body on the astral plane. Our emotional bodies here on the Earth plane represent the amount of light we are able to wield into existence. In other words: how we feel is directly proportional to how much light we are carrying on a daily basis. Theoretically, if the light scale was one to ten, with one being masculine energy (representing expansion and force) and ten being feminine energy (representing contraction and form), we can fall anywhere on that scale depending on the demand of our current light state. There are *only* two types of humans that are born: ones with male sex organs and ones with female sex organs; our energetic states, however, dictate how we identify on an infinite spectrum of emotion (i.e., levels of masculinity or femininity). These energetic states go beyond male/female physical body parts *given* at birth. Masculine energy is associated with force, the giving aspect. Feminine energy is associated with form, the receiving aspect. Both aspects are needed to create harmony and balance within humanity.

In addition to the creation of life, creating can also come in infinite forms and expressions of these two energy states working in unison. The state of our light body determines the state of our emotional body, thereby transcending our emotional intelligence. With this awareness, I can let go of labels of separation and instead think of it as an organized energy. I am not only a physical body. I am a vast array of light energy constantly in motion, seeking my source of good, and allowing it to inspire my movement. The amount of inner freedom these revelations inspire within my being allows for astral travel among other high-vibrational light energies.

This is an exploration of heavenly light. The life activation awareness began unfolding mysteries in new ways as I became more self-aware. In light of my profound experiences, becoming a life activation practitioner was the natural next step in the path of enlightenment. I wanted others to experience the ultimate reality of the big picture. With my shamanic wand in hand, I would step into total service to the Hierarchy of Light as a life activation practitioner.

THE SECRET KNOWLEDGE OF MIRACLES IN SESSION

Svaha!

As I moved into a new role of being both the giver and receiver of the flow of light, I was filled with an even deeper desire to increase my understanding of God. Going within to the inner light connected me to a higher light and intelligence. I call this God consciousness. God consciousness allowed for a magnification of the God potentiality in me. Marvelous. This was a sizable shift in consciousness: God as my source of good. Prior to the psychic change, I considered my place of employment as "my source" of income. I had focused on my career through a life-or-death mentality because it was my "my source" of income. I considered the relationship I was in with my career as "my source" of security. I considered my yoga practice "my source" of well-being. I gave people, places, and events (that I was pulling "my source" from) all my power.

I had pulled all my power from external things (the very definition of bondage of self), because I served the ego.

These "outside sources" were equivalent to the metaphor of existing in my own home, but when I was thirsty, I would go out the front door, walk to the neighbor's house, and ask them for a glass of water. I would stand at the neighbor's house, knocking and knocking, and if there was no answer, I would go to *their* neighbors and ask for a glass of water. There, I would stay knocking away until someone would eventually come to the door and give me water. I was unaware of the possibility of an inner dwelling within my own home. A person unaware of their inner dwelling is a *homeless* person. Where there is homeless, there is hopeless. This is a conditioned state; it is not natural. I was sitting on a can of infinite possibilities, Divine love, all the security one could ever wish for, unbeknownst to me. Sitting on my inner can with my hat out, counting on the things outside of me to come through for me. I would sing, dance, and perform all kinds of circus acts to get the attention of *where I thought* my good would come from—and it was always secondhand. From my ego-centered state, I defined this hardworking tactic as "go-getter." The irony of the story of the beggar is that he eventually falls over dead, and when he does, the rusted can he sat on his entire life opens, and out comes a bundle of gold. Gold symbolizing the riches of life. My insanity (making outside things my source of income) would be the breaking point in the psychic change. Until I came to believe I am missing nothing. I already *am* it all. I already have it all. The *all* is my true source; the riches of my God consciousness became available.

Where there is insanity, there is suffering. I was experiencing insanity through constant acts of going outside of myself to meet my needs. I would get home at night and feel accomplished after having finally found that glass of water through feelings of desperation for survival. As you can imagine, this was a lot of hard work. It also kept me out of the miracle of life because I lived in a state where I couldn't enjoy anything until "the water was conquered." Everything was a means to an end. There was no journey enjoyment; instead, there was a lot of self-pity for having to work so hard. Although, I am grateful for my entire journey, because this was my path to discovery—I hope this book and this message can serve as a channel of inspiration to understanding the God consciousness awaiting recognition within each of us. I hope that my experiences and my words will help you avoid the insanity of going outside yourself any further to discover your riches.

Coming to believe in our God consciousness is an evolutionary process afforded to us as we carry our God consciousness. Through this practice, I came to believe there is no such thing as necessary suffering. I do not believe in suffering at all. Our path is our path, and those unenlightened decisions I made prior to being given the opportunity for atonement were symbiotic to my soul journey. My soul knows the most direct path to my enlightenment (full ego deflation), and every element of life came together for the perfect dissolution. The old ideas attached to the suffering didn't work. I had managed my suffering for so long that I didn't even realize I was suffering in a sober state. I didn't realize where I was going to take a hit off the old story (the old belief system) to keep that old idea intact, thereby keeping me suffering in that area of my life. Carrying the God consciousness revealed these very intimate (as in "in-to-me-see") directions. I had a choice to not participate in the habitual ways of being, the mindless action. I carried the power to make a new choice, and so it was.

TITHING

Prior to the psychic change, I held the idea that I didn't have enough income to tithe my money. Certainly, if I am suffering from the ignorance that I am responsible for the good in my life, then the core belief *I am not enough* is sure to follow. When *I am not enough*, I hold the idea that *I don't have enough*, and giving up the little bit I do have seems daunting. The ignorance is being unaware that all good comes from the Law of Good. The Law of Good becomes active as soon as I accept my godliness. The Law of Good is constantly working for me, even if I reject it, thereby rejecting my godliness. By rejecting its presence, I'm basically using my human will to negate its flow. I'm saying, *No, thank you, God, I prefer to live life in lack without your love. I choose to judge those who have your grace and maintain my prejudices about things I don't understand.* This is living in the arrogance of ignorance.

The true exercise of my faith is believing that all good comes from the Law of Good, and that it is ever-flowing, always abundant, and *loving.* In this knowingness, we gladly give of our time, treasures, and talents, as well as our sincerest appreciations for the portal of light (the godliness flowing to and from us). When we have sincerely admitted complete defeat and abandoned ourselves to the One, the delightful healing that arrives from the Hierarchy of Light is greater than what can be felt on the Earthly plane. We know it's something greater than ourselves and we become willing to do whatever it takes to maintain our connection to it. The connection supersedes our other priorities. It is so loving to have such a relationship with the One that we are willing to give what has been so freely given unto us. The heavy "goings" of life are rooted in human will only, which activates the negative ego (which highlights erroneous core beliefs). In this blocked state of mind, body, and soul, I certainly was not seeking spiritual guidance with tithing from a foundation of truth. In this ego-centered state, I sought spiritual guidance based only on *self*. People knew where I personally tithed because I told them, if I even tithed at all.

On the path of self-seeking (the ego-centered state), if I didn't receive information from others that further supported my self-centeredness, then no problem. I would just character assassinate them in my mind and move on. I had a story about everything and everyone who didn't cosign my ego. If there was something I liked, though? Then I would employ what worked and leave the rest behind. I treated my self-seeking like a fusion program. In my mind, I was the most truthful *always*; however, my understanding of truth was as simple as noting that I hadn't told a lie that day, or if I did tell a lie, it was a white lie and those didn't count. When I made these silly agreements within my mind, next came the experience of grandiosity for being truthful. LOL. The truth was this was the only "kind of truth" available to me being outside of my God consciousness. I would do things and not get caught. In my *hopeless* state, if I didn't get caught it was like it never happened. The countless times I lied to myself added up. When I lied to myself, I lied the loudest. The inner dialogue of *I didn't hurt anybody because I was the only one there* was reinforcing the idea that I didn't count. I wasn't counting myself. The only consciousness I was responsible for was the one I was carrying, and the Law of Good doesn't miss one belief, thought, or action in and out of God consciousness.

It was time to honor my true source of all things. It was time to tithe in faith and be free of living paycheck to paycheck. It was time to stop measuring self-worth based on the balance of my bank account. It was time to make a new decision around tithing—I was ready to test my God consciousness in the area of tithing. After all, having to wait to tithe, and wait to show my appreciation for the good I was receiving, seemed counterproductive to what I innately knew was being told to me in meditation. I was the idea of God. God came before all things. My tithing would come before all things. Accepting my godliness meant being a host of God. I *am a personal expression* of God, my good comes from God, and I *am* enough and have more than enough to serve my life contract and the people around me. It never ends. *Boom!* Every single penny that arrived, I began to give my tenth to God off the top, and then let God decide where it would go. Ten percent of every dollar, no matter how it came to me, I tithed. Not only did this strengthen my connection to God through my inner portal, it manifested true independence as I was now dependent from within (versus outside). God could count on me, and I could count on God. God kept promises and tithing gave me the power to keep promises too. This strengthened my relationship with God and with others. This was a surrendering of my finances to God; I was being restored to sanity in my finances, and it was good.

Applying faith in the spiritual principle of tithing boldly activated magnetic forces into my life. *Letting go* was *ultimate* magnetism. My giving, regardless of what outcomes I could fathom, allowed me to let go of my faulty beliefs and prejudices about money. The old story of the haves and have-nots was no more. These revelations paralleled my revelations about time: We all come from God, and we all return to God. All money comes from God, and all money returns to God. Tithing was a direct experience with God. "God willing" was revealed. At that moment, all limiting beliefs about money dissolved. Poof. Gone. The sunlight of the Spirit flowed in, and light energy was magnified within me even more. My reliance on God was tenfold!

There is a secret to the recipe of tithing: we ought to give our tenth to where we are truly receiving our spiritual guidance if we hope to keep that channel illuminating our path. This is what it means to stand on the shoulders of giants. It's those who came before us, who have courageously walked the illuminated path with dignity. We give to those giants who've accepted their godliness and lived serving the Hierarchy of Light. The giants are those who have mastered their light here on the Earth plane. When I gave in this way, the return was plentiful. Tenfold, a hundredfold, a thousandfold, returns, further developing my trust fund.

FORGIVENESS

Living in God's grace is living in a state of being forgiven. It's the human will that is unable to forgive. God's will is forgiveness. Once I become aware of harm caused by any means, I forgive. Forgiveness ought to come instinctively through grace. It is by God forgiving me that I have the power to forgive. Why? This is because, after the psychic change, I now seek the God in everything. In seeking the God in it, I am able to see, sympathize, empathize, and be with the wrongdoing in a state of peace. I can see the person, place, or thing with my God consciousness. I can forgive first and offer love. Most acts of harm are a cry for love. The application of love is the correct response in the mind. By blessing people and situations with forgiveness, I am using my God consciousness to remove the harm and, in doing so, breaking the negative emotional bonds of resentment, getting even, and anger. The hurts in the mind manifest as hurts in the body. There is no room for God's grace in a hurt mind. The hurt mind is clouded. The clouded mind blocks off the flow of God's grace. Hurt in the mind creates a victim state (a state of no rights or freedom) where we are suffering from a lack consciousness, which is the staging ground for negative ego. We are confused about how God's law works. The lack of forgiveness produces guilt, shame, and self-pity. Always forgive first. Know all is well.

The Law of Good works for us, in Divine order, with Divine flow. In accepting our godliness, we think from our belief of being connected to the One Who Has All Power and All Knowledge. We then act accordingly, in alignment with God's will. This provides for a faith foundation where all things sustainable manifest. Here, our response to life is always from within, as we take responsibility for what we see and are willing to uphold through the Law of Good. We acquire full vision, and the "veil of distortion" falls away.

With the entire universe happening for me, there is constant feedback revealing to me my state of being. A disagreement is an opportunity to apply love and forgive. This is my part. This is what I can do, and this is what I instinctively do to keep the God consciousness I am carrying alive and well. I get to see your fullness now because I myself am full. The root of forgiveness is wholeness. Forgiveness is the experience of connectedness in pure form. I can only see what I believe, that's it. If I see what's right with you, I myself am right.

THE THING IS NOT THE THING

The mind creates delusions in duality that make us believe that we are separate: separated from God, and therefore separated from each other. Separateness always reveals itself by exposing an outside threat. For example, something outside of myself "appears" to be threatening my well-being. In this confusion, I am not seeing the God in another. I am seeing a threat, and *this is the lie.* In our wholeness, nothing outside of us can change our wholeness—*unless* we allow the ego to personalize it by creating a story around it, and then we agree with the story. This is where stereotypes, prejudices, and biases of all kinds enter. We must see this lie for what it is, and then surrender it to our understanding of a power greater than ourselves.

Outside help from a spiritual guide has one purpose: to assist in helping us "GODIRECT."

We must GODIRECT by tilling our soil until our seeds sprout. In helping others, I must hear those magic words, "I need your help." Otherwise, I must be willing to take my own advice. So in the face of projection (what I think you should do), I take my own suggestions. In the application of my suggestion, I am *God willing*. As the solution arrives in my consciousness, if it's good enough for whatever I am about to project it on, then it's good enough for me. I must be actively practicing my suggestion for you *right now*. In my connectedness, I no longer give it all away. That would be the practice of not feeling worthy of the solution and not fully understanding projection. Consciousness is contagious. It exists across past, present, and future versions of myself. As I actively take my own suggestions, the Law of Good takes care of everything else. Our combined tangible results speak volumes.

Life is a mirror of perception. We see who we are in others. We attract what we are. When I told my relationship stories, the plots had a central theme: what *happened* to me. My stories were glamorous dramas. I was at the center of a drama that lasted many episodes. I was the victim in my relations with others, no matter how colorful the circumstances were. Equally important to my perception of "what happened to me" was that my sense of well-being was tied to these disasters. Things like embarrassment and shame for not having achieved a "full life" was my experience. From this separated vibration, I was experiencing the attitude of false pride. Anytime there is action out of denial (denying my connection to God consciousness), pride will not allow me to come clean. Denial and pride go hand in hand. We have the right to be wrong. I held the belief that I was undeserving of a full life. The only thing worse than being wrong (denial) was staying wrong (pride), so admitting complete defeat AND asking for God's help became my superpower.

I came to believe that each day when the sun rises, I am new. I would admit complete defeat over my mind, body, and affairs. I would invite the Hierarchy of Light into my day, and ask it to direct me. *How can I best serve Thee?* In the area of personal relations, this was not easy coming from a life built on negative ego. However, with this type of surrender, I was emptying my cup. I began to tap into a subtle current of consciousness, and I began to get out of my own way, freed of old ideas and habitual ways of being.

When we get to tap into this subtle current, the revelations of God come, and *we listen*. Observing the core belief for what it is and without judgment allows it to pass through. Allowing ourselves a grieving process is healthy. Allowing ourselves the emotion of sadness is our Divine right. Emotions are beautiful, and we experience the correct emotion for the action performed, and thus we are in balance. Meeting ourselves in the depths of our darkness is called grieving by bringing our God consciousness; our sober, full awareness to these feelings gives rise out of denial and up the ladder to anger, bargaining, resignation, and acceptance. The birth of the moment arrives where I can truly demonstrate my understanding of the principle of projection. Until then, principle remains knowledge-based only. It remains in its potential state waiting to be observed. By giving it my observation, by taking my own advice, I allow the application of the principle to set matters straight. My life was on repeat, and I had continued relying on survival skills as a way of life—until being humbled by the acceptance of my godliness. Acceptance was the key to a new invisible door. It was by arriving at acceptance that I became ready to do whatever it took to relieve my habitual way of being for uncharted spiritual territories.

WHAT IS AMEN?

"Amen" is the root word for amends. Amen means I believe. Making amends is an action we take to restore relations with others once we restore our internal governments. When we have come to the realization of projection, and how we project either our faith or our fear onto the canvas of life—we can easily accept our part in every circumstance, seeing it as an opportunity for growth. We learn that we create the world(s) we live in, and as we align our internal governments, it is only natural that we return to the people and places we have harmed in order to mend the relations.

The act of amends proceeds forward to heal things "that happened to us" as a result of our negative core beliefs that have separated us from our God consciousness. By seeking God in the amends process, and asking for guidance, we can make a plan of action. Our plan of action has a foundation of faith: we trust God. We carry honesty, open-mindedness, and willingness in the amends process. The amends process is an act of bringing our consciousness current. Taking responsibility for when we were unaware and disconnected in mind from God. This tedious training sets us up for a lifetime of participating in the grace of forgiveness. To my inner light, I can ask, *Who am I in honesty with this situation?* In my seeking of honesty through meditation (where I actively seek my inner light), I can listen in order to become one with the amends process. When I set out to amend harm caused by my actions, I am making peace with that inner pain, giving it the healing of forgiveness. With God's help, it dissipates.

In our progression through higher consciousness, our amends change form. It is *a healing power,* an act of something greater than ourselves. Making amends can seem daunting to the ego, and if this is the case, I can pray for the willingness to move forward in making these amends. The amends process is literally like a lamp lighting the path for our feet to stay grounded. When done with a sincere heart (i.e., we really do want to make it better, we really do want to own our part), then forgiveness enters into the process like never before.

Forgiveness is a shift in consciousness, and through the process of amends, we begin to live forgiveness and experience a greater force of love. Amen is a way of making our claim on the universal mind, the mind of God, in absolute truth. It is an offering of ourselves to God in an equation of multiplying good. It is a space of sacredness we claim within our godliness *for* godliness. It is completing right action, and then letting go, knowing that our part is done. It's ensuring togetherness. It is being restored to our original condition, then, with effortless flow, sharing our wholeness for the good of *all*. It is above and beyond healing.

We can also say amen after a single prayer as a way of accepting "the done deal." We can use amen as a mantra to center our mind with our soul. The amen spiritual tool is infinite in nature, and when used in a sacred circle—it becomes a covenant to pick up our God duties and let God decide. Making amends opens the door to humility: *the gem of life*. It implies a change in behavior and the adoption of attitudes and actions.

As we progress into higher consciousness, our amends become silent prayers for others. When I encounter a troubled person in my mind or in my reality, I begin to pray for them. I pray for their well-being, their joy, and for a life to be given unto them beyond their wildest dreams. I pray for their connection to spirit, for the infinite portal to open, and for the miracle of life to come into their life like never before. I do this until peace returns. This is a great way to practice humility: doing for others without being found out.

THE ART OF PRAYER

The foundation of faith is quintessential for emotional transformation to take root and develop within us in magnificent, glorious ways. I had been solely focused on developing the foundation of faith with God for several years. God was my soul mate, and I knew this through and through. I was in full surrender, *all of life* in God's hands. Going within to my inner light (my inner portal) to ask for God's help was instinctive. Letting go of the expectations of outcomes, the expectations of my will, the drive of self-centeredness—opened a new door to inner freedom.

My research with prayer as a spiritual formula for success led me to the study of the therapeutic effects of intercessory prayer completed in 2001 by Leonard Leibovici, MD. The study was a retroactive intervention where half a group of patients suffering from illness were prayed for by a blind prayer group. The blind prayer group was only given instructions to pray for half of the group in 2001. What the blind prayer group didn't know was that the group they were praying for had been suffering from their illness between 1991 and 1996. In the compilation of the study, the statistics showed that the group that was prayed for, even though they had been ill four to ten years prior, showed significant changes in their health condition in 2001.[1] In addition to the power of prayer working in the past, prayer also worked in future events. Prayer, being a spiritual principle and infinite in nature, had reached beyond time and space. The spiritual principle of prayer didn't delineate time. Prayer's power healed past, present, and future as one moment. Quintessence.

---

1. Leonard Leibovici, "Effects of Remote, Retroactive Intercessory Prayer on Outcomes in Patients with Bloodstream Infection: Randomised Controlled Trial," *British Medical Journal* 323 (December 22, 2001): 1450, www.bmj.com/content/323/7327/1450.

When I prayed, I altered myself in what I perceived as the "past me," I altered myself in what I perceived as the "future me," and I uplifted the "present me." In deep contemplation of this content, I came to believe that whatever I prayed for, I could bless and praise the trauma right out of existence. It would dissolve completely and fully in past, present, and future versions of myself. There is only one me, and that me responds to the art of prayer. This is the meaning of "quantum possibilities." Praying with a sincere heart brought forth miraculous occurrences. Praying ritually manifests healings right in front of my face, one at a time. I began praying for others—everything I would have for myself. I began blessing and praising *all*, especially the things I thought were nuances. I spent many days blessing children as well. By blessing children, I was also blessing my inner child, the one who so desperately needed my love and protection. What did blessing and praising children have to do with what I was up against in the present? I was a projection of my childhood trauma in the suffering state—blessing children became the *catalyst* of my growth. They were me.

I spent day after day blessing and praising all elements of life. Then I would use my imagination to see myself in the light, doing what I love, feeling healed, combined with the things that brought me joy. I imagined thriving children in healthy homes receiving all of my answered prayers with grace. I used my imagination from the first person to truly envision life beyond my wildest dreams: enchanted fairy-tale castles in the sky, space travel, and so much more. The highest version of joy was available to me in my imagination, and soon it would appear in my reality. Serenity and peace were my riches. I was healthily rich!

As I began to heal from within with these prayers and visualizations, I literally watched the transformation of my new life unfold right before my eyes. I continued to surrender to God's will with humility, honesty, and forgiveness in imagination.

I begin again every day in the likeness of God, *for* God, *with* God. The art of prayer was a superpower.

Striving to become aligned with spiritual principles, and then allowing our alignment to guide us in our best versions of ourselves, is perfection. In this relationship with success, we already are successful. Our intentions originate from a place of wholeness. Our motive is to find out how we can use our greatest God-given talents and gifts, and how we can be an asset to God's creation for the good of all. In this, we are free of expectations and results. We are committed to doing a great job for our Creator, and we treat each mission like a trillion-dollar client, because we have internalized where our good comes from. We have learned the art of being human. We admit complete defeat and ask for God's help. We invite God into each situation. We are ready to enjoy our life's experiences, and we get to engage our passions without pulling our sense of self-worth from them. Our relations and activities are no longer life-or-death; instead, our relations are restored—because we are restored. We enter life each morning right-sized and ready for anything.

CHAPTER 6

THE SPIRITUAL PRINCIPLE OF ONENESS

I am God.

People will tell you exactly where they are emotionally: just listen up and be humbled through your hearing. The lower emotional states like sloth, hoarding, jealousy, and gossiping are derived from our lower selves—and the higher emotional states like kindness, serenity, love, and joy are derived from our higher self-experience. To know one of these is to know its polar opposite. When we are separated from our inner portal to God, there is nowhere else for us to go except into the lower self-nature of our ego. This separation happens in the mind, because no soul structure can ever be separated from its source, and all parts of the human are held together by what we know on this planet as gravity—but the mind can create the illusion of separation, and this can go on indefinitely.

The nature of the lower self is never feeling that it is enough, which is why we are constantly pulling our power from outside things to overcompensate for lower self-inadequacy. The core beliefs, born out of being separated from God, are *I am not enough, I am unworthy, I am unlovable,* and *I am alone.* These beliefs will never create the sustainable ecosystems required to build our internal governments. Our internal governments insist on being highly organized in spirit, soul, and physical form in order to sustain us emotionally while simultaneously holding the *power to integrate* the expressions of our Godliness. The all-powerful *I am* is a spiritual principle that can only be activated in alignment with God's will. It is a key to a new freedom and a new happiness that only fits in the door of humility. Without humility, humans only have access to the small *I am* because it is the egoic mind that is attempting to use the key. The highest level an egoic mind can reach is the top of performance principles. Remember the performance principles are of the world and have an end point; there is no eternal value associated with them. They are good as far as they go. It's beautiful how God's design keeps humility as the solid expression and hidden key for the eternal evolutionary journey.

Inside, we are already a whole world. We are whole and complete, and it is our responsibility to be the gatekeeper of our world. We accept this responsibility by accepting the fact that we are God. We are One. The One that is in me is the One that is in you. One is God. God is One. Our interconnectedness to each other is our Godliness. In the conscious decision to align our human will with God's will (which is *already* within us), we awaken to the responsibility of life. We awaken that Sleepy Hollow tree that lay over us in bondage. Our new tree of life swirls around us in the form of light energy, regenerating, nourishing, and pouring love right into our golden roots. Like the first sight of spring in an enchanted forest, our DNA codes dance with light, color, and creativity. We then have the power to build our worlds with the sophistication of our God consciousness.

Some of us have this lie of separation sealed so tightly that even if it was brought to our attention with tangible evidence, we'd be shocked by it. The lower self would be shocked, then offended—then, based on our willingness to heal, could reject the whole idea because of the *misinterpretation* of time. Remember from our prayer teachings that all of the spiritual principles are infinite in nature—meaning they go beyond time. Time is something we have here on the Earth plane for organization. We are infinite beings, and when we appropriate spiritual principles, our intention can alter our existence. We saw this with the powerful use of prayer. In our prayers, we have the ability to bless and praise things, and in doing so, we bring those things into the light in new, glorious ways. Praying has infinite healing capabilities. Praying is an intelligence beyond our human understanding.

We get to experience the phenomenon of prayer in our "God willing." Our God willing is *us/one/God/we*. God is who we are. We are God. I am God. Willing is action. "Willing" in Latin means to wish. Action equals God. *Us/one/God/we* is who we are. This is our being. This is what it means to be. In this knowingness, our willingness comes alive. Our wishes come alive. Our tree of life comes alive. Our trees wield power, and our yields harvest abundantly. Amen.

It's really hard to see ourselves and take responsibility for who we are in the moment. Becoming willing to do this takes true faith (believing in the unseen), true trust (believing I can count on it), and true courage (believing God in me is majority), no matter what! Once a powerful seed of our Godliness is planted within, once we become curious about what we believe, and once we have the slightest idea that there could be more to life than what meets the eye—we open ourselves up to the ultimate reality awaiting us. When we awaken to our ability to draw upon the Source—being a God is like discovering an invisible door with a mysterious lock. After decades of seeking the key, you suddenly discover that only *your fingerprints* can open it; this is because—you are the key! We must do it for ourselves first. The Source, with my willingness, is the only thing that can open the door—at just the right time and in just the right way. Our light energy responds magnificently to its intelligence, in which light magnifies itself in ways that activate our talents and gifts. There, our completeness is revealed.

We learn transmutation of the lower self through our meditation and devotion to the Law of Good, the Hierarchy of Light, and the Source. We push through portals of the veil of distortion. In our application of channeling our lower nature into something positive, our force and our form find balance. Instead of reacting to a perceived threat, we choose a creative response through our connection with our inner light. In our continuous efforts, a bridge across the abyss is formed where no bridge existed before. A bridge from nothingness into somethingness across an abyss that once ruled our existence. Now, at the perimeters of our spiritual landscape, like the abstract chaos of a fiery sky at sunset, we get to walk the rainbow bridge, the light beam! The light beam carries us home. It is always magical to catch a rainbow. Let it be so.

Assisting others through this process is the greatest expression of being human. We get to have a front-row seat to the spiritual awakenings of others. We get to experience the leveling-up process within them. The light we carry magnifies as we continue our process of light mastery. Our humanoid system becomes an attuned antenna for the Law of Good. It corresponds to the spheres of light that lay on top of our energetic existence. We are no longer threatened by external happenings. We have the power to bring forth peaceful solutions. We have the power to unify opposing forces. We have the power to stabilize emotions and achieve victory over them.

We have the power of understanding, and the power to love others—our fellow godheads.

We carry the power as creators. We carry the willing nature of God. In alignment with God's will within us, we serve the One Who Has All Power and All Knowledge. That which created us/God and gave us/God a soul, a spirit, and a consciousness. This is the One beyond what our limited humanism can fathom—but it is there. Accepting the responsibility of our life contract expands our understanding of our Godliness. We have the potential of God consciousness. With the adoption of rightly aligned action, we transmute and level up. Accepting the responsibility of our life contract expands our inner freedom and our truest understanding of freedom—which, in turn, produces more humility: the gem of life.

ACCEPTANCE AFFIRMATION

Infinite intelligence is the Source of my supply.

My entire trust is in infinite intelligence.

There are many ways in which my good comes to me.

All ways spring open from the rich source of abundant good.

I accept *I am God.*

I take full responsibility for my life.

I accept my God consciousness here, now.

Daily, I meditate on the Source.

How can I best serve Thee?

My channels are open, and *I am richly blessed.*

Amen.

In this new paradise where our superpowers return, we live in humility. Our divinity by birth returns to us. We are expected to use our God power in alignment with the Source. Spiritual tools come with a great responsibility of service. Service is the act of assisting others in understanding their Godliness. We become assets to the Law of Good through service. We perform tasks of all kinds in the great work of human evolution. The efficacy of our internal work shines through the ecosystems we participate in as trusted servants. Talents and gifts activated, we are in world service.

SCRATCHING THE SURFACE

Sacred geometry is how we describe both the math and the art-science of creation. The Hermetic axiom "As above, so below" refers to sacred geometry as it connects heaven to Earth. In other words, its "here-now" patterns itself across all dimensions. We think of heaven as being above because the elevating nature of our consciousness is drawn up in our lightness. The elevating nature of our consciousness happens as the organization of our light energy takes place (the light energy within us and all around us).

As we ascend in consciousness, we get to experience greater portions of creation. This is made so by the release of our emotional baggage associated with negative core beliefs that live like viruses in the mind. We experience an emotion, and in our experience, it seems as if the emotion has a look—but the emotion itself has no look; we give the formless energy form when we decide what it is. All sustenance has intelligence, and it is through our humanoid system that processes its intelligence that we get to have an experience. We are connected to the heavens through spheres of energy that are mathematically organized throughout the creation of Earth.

The more we observe these particles and give them our attention, the more intelligence flows from them that is infinite, as well as intimate, to our fingerprints. These spheres of energy are everywhere and come out of nothingness. From the black dot on the back of the ladybug to the stripes of a zebra, the patterns of geometry repeat themselves in infinite form throughout nature. Everywhere we look, they can be found. When they manifest, they do so by following precise formulas. The spheres carry intelligence. The intelligence is discovering itself. While in sacred space (a space defined by Divine union), we bridge the space between heaven and Earth, making it one, making it *now*. We are integrating our soul, spirit, and consciousness into *one* via *ujjayi pranayama*, the Sanskrit word for "breath of life," or "life force." Becoming masters of light asks something huge of us: the request of namaste. The Sanskrit word "namaste," which means "I bow to [the inner light in] you," relates to *imago Dei*, or "image of God" in Latin. Thus, we bow to it.

CONTENT OF CHARACTER

Prior to the psychic change (the awareness of a shift in my consciousness), I bought into all kinds of suppressing marketing. Sayings I often heard from my peers and the "cosigners" of my lower-natured self (you know, the people I gathered to support me in my lie) were those like "pick your poison," or "everyone has one vice." Catchphrases like this kept me buried in self-pity. I fell victim to the mental illness of thoughts such as *Nobody is going to find out* or *This isn't hurting anyone because I am the only one involved.* It took a lot of work once I became sober (complete and total abstinence from alcohol and other mind-altering substances) to truly take the seat of my soul.

I began to see that because of who I was, I was attracting the very opposite of the miracle of life. What I was hearing were sayings that supported *the lie of separateness*, which is where I was living spiritually, emotionally, and consciously. I was in a self-fulfilled prophecy of *less than* existence. With this understanding, I had to admit complete defeat in my habitual way of being and thinking. I needed help to rearrange my internal government (the world we are responsible for). In this surrendering state (admission of complete defeat in all things), everything fell away.

This was scary stuff as my public appearance (the negative ego leading my life) was at stake. Everything I thought I was responsible for was falling away right in front of my eyes. Everything I had known, every tactic, every strategy to survive—was no longer available to me in this demolition of falsehood. A new state of consciousness was being born, a oneness that supported the apex of nothingness. Even if I acted out in those old ways of being out of rote memory, the action dissolved itself in its delivery. Like a hose being turned off at the source, the water trickling until it was no more. It was like the cycle of a full-on laughing fit: first, the deep belly laugh, then straight laughter, then more laughing, then repeating the joke to keep the laughter going—until the joke has been appreciated for all of its comedy—and finally, you take a breath as you wipe the tears away and say, "Whew, *that* was funny!" The show was over; the curtain was closed. The new tools: honesty, faith, love, and courage had a heartbeat, and when I took my next breaths, I breathed in the qualities of life—and *they* breathed me in.

The "it" responsiveness began, and a life beyond my wildest dreams commenced. I did what I was supposed to do because I *wanted* to. I had access to the Law of Good, and I knew my part. I let go of *why* and instead said, "Thank you." I began treating everyone like a trillion-dollar client because everyone and everything was. I was giving my absolute best to every opportunity, and when my work was done, I forgot all about it. Each morning, I would rise and empty my cup. I would admit complete defeat in all of my affairs (in case there was any residual success I was still clinging to). All success was far more God's than mine. In this surrender, I could open myself up to the ultimate intelligence and be used by the Hierarchy of Light in the master program of life where *I am intelligence* becoming a human being.

Memories flashed through my software, my consciousness, as it continued to purify itself. Through this, I became acutely aware of the old software programming I was carrying. When I told myself *nobody would find out*, what I was really saying was *I don't count.* I wasn't counting myself. I was the only one I was responsible for, and yet I kept leaving myself out of the equation. I couldn't *see* me. I could only see you. I could see exactly the way in which *you* ought to do it. Seeing how *you* should do something was my greatest sign from the canvas of life. The "it" continued to show me through others. I was carrying the old software, the consciousness of not being self-aware—that's it. I was generating the fear of being left behind from not including myself. This was all self-inflicted. Each time I would take part in my conditioned response to "my only vice," or the mass marketing of mediocrity—I was not confronting what needed to be confronted. With a lifetime of going outside of myself to meet my basic needs, there was a lifetime of living behind a smoke screen. Ironically, I was a person who tried to keep my cigarette-smoking habit from others throughout the physical manifestation of that. I had dysfunctional, suppressing behaviors of all kinds driving me to death. As this passed through my consciousness in its finale, with complete surrender, I shouted out: *"I matter!"* And so it was.

Dang! Spirit, Divine mind, and ultimate intelligence are right here, right now, with me. Everything and everyone is accounted for in the master program of life. There was no one hiding; there was no one kept in the dark. Nothingness knew everything, and I reported directly to the Creator as a Creator God on the Earth plane.

LOVE HAS NO OPPOSITE

Letting go completely came in the fall of 2018 when the Woolsey Fire came through Malibu, California. I departed from my home in the early morning on November 11 for a simple day trip, flying clients up the California coast. My home, situated at the top of Corral Canyon, was at the end of a three-mile winding drive, and the wind was howling on this particular morning. The winds were so strong that boulders had fallen and cracked open onto the mountain road. The sun rising over the mountains, its rays spread out over the ocean, was impeccably beautiful. The casted shadows upon certain curves in the road, however, made it increasingly difficult to see the dispersed sharp rocks. I was doing my best to avoid them to prevent a tire puncture, but by the time I got to the bottom of the hill, I had two flat tires.

To the best of my ability, I pulled the car off to the side of the Pacific Coast Highway. It was in a safe place, and I was satisfied with leaving it there in order to be on time for my flight from Van Nuys Airport. There was no time to call for help, and the flat tires were not an emergency. I would deal with them after my flight day, when my commitment was complete. I called an Uber, and due to the quickness of finding a solution, I was still early for the flight. As the captain, arriving at the airplane first was good form. I liked to greet our team one by one when they arrived. Checking in with each colleague would set the tone for our safe day. The camaraderie between a flight crew is second to none. I took this very seriously.

Other than the adventure of the morning, the passengers were on time, and all other elements of our flight flowed seamlessly. During our takeoff, the crew resource callouts were as planned:

> Positive rate (check).
> Gear up (check).
> Four hundred feet (check).
> Flaps up. Manual speed 200 kts. Flight level change (check).

Although we were in a sterile cockpit (a stage of flight where we observe silence and essential communication only categorized by our altitude below ten thousand feet), the copilot decided that the smoke-filled skies moving toward Malibu were worthy of mentioning. During sterile cockpit, only talk related to the performance of our roles and the safety of the aircraft is allowed—that's it! Our full awareness is dedicated to safely maneuvering the aircraft out of the airport environment and into the above airspace with precise determination. The copilot muttered, "The fire perimeter for the city of Malibu and surrounding counties was just enforced."

Acknowledging what he said, I replied, "Copy." Of course, this sent my mind into a reverse course over my morning. My home was in Malibu. I had only packed a day bag for this flight. The items I chose were workout clothes and my running shoes. I had my laptop, my toiletries kit, and my flying documents: passport, medical certificates, and pilot's license. However, my car and my house and a lifetime of around-the-world heirlooms were in the set perimeter. The sequence of events of my morning played in reverse in my mind as I came to the conclusion that my entire life was within that perimeter! I released a pained chuckle.

Air traffic control gave us a heading, directing our path of flight around the smoke-filled skies until we were on a northerly heading with both the airport and Malibu behind us. At ten thousand feet, I took a deep breath—and like an unexpected death happening without the pleasure of getting to say goodbye, I silently let go. Uncharted territory began. The timing of the universe was exact, and all I could feel was love.

With the *love* I was carrying, I got right into service helping others. The world got to watch the raging fires from afar as they cleared 96,949 acres of land, our homes, and lifetimes of memories. A gigantic amount of love kept flowing into my consciousness. I did my absolute best to channel the love into my service with others. I did my absolute best to stay in a positive attitude no matter what was going on externally. I positioned myself an hour south of the fire devastation where I could be a nobody. I had $2,500 in my bank account. I withdrew a tenth, $250, and tithed it right away. I chose to tithe to a spiritual teacher I had grown to love. I knew that I ought to tithe where I was receiving my spiritual guidance. I knew my source was God, and God was infinite. The tithe was an instinctual demonstration of my faith.

This was essential to keep the Law of Good flowing into my consciousness. I understood that what I focused on, gave my awareness to, and placed value on would expand. I placed my entire reliance on God with faith that God would deliver. Every single one of my thoughts, my actions, and my exchanges with others counted. This was secret knowledge that had been handed down to me through my seeking of higher consciousness. I had read about it in hundreds of spiritual books. It'd been explained many different ways, but the efficacy of my tithe was sure to return tenfold. I served others in humble circles where people were recovering from alcoholism. I kept saying to myself, *I can't wait to see what good comes from this.* I continued to focus on the miracles of the day, and how I could best serve Thee.

Because of the years of determination it took to confront the difficulties of my life—to take responsibility, to overcome a lifetime of going outside of myself to meet my basic needs, and to live in the spiritual experience as a way of life—when one of the worst natural disasters California had ever seen arrived, I had the power to observe it with grace. The sacrifice of my negative ego in every moment, one moment at a time, had yielded the fruit of *love*. Love is riches.

Thirty days had passed. Christmas was here, and I was on a flight mission to bring the victims of the fires donated gift bags. Gift bags that were filled with goods of all kinds. Our flight crew was delivering goods and services to families that had lost everything. In the midst of giving hugs and sharing heartfelt smiles, it dawned on me that I was one of them. I had completely forgotten that I was a victim of the fire. In fact, my mind never even went there. I was so immersed in helping others and focusing on the miracles of the day, one day at a time, that I was lifted in pure *love*.

The more I served, the more *true love* flowed into my life. I could serve without preference. I could fly the aircraft, if that was what I was called to do. I could help victims to safety, if that was what I was called to do. I could let go of my worldly attachments, if that was what I was called to do. In *love, the call* was the opportunity. In humility, I had become a leader attuned to the way of the whole. I was free.

HALLELUJAH, WHAT'S IT TO YOU?

Well, well, well, we come to the end of this sacred exchange together! Moving through the gravity portal we all pass through—entering into life and our wonderful wizardry ways—we sometimes find each other to hear *just one word* in a new way. Our evolutionary human experiences of discovering knowledge, taking action, and perceiving our tangible results allow us to build worlds of sustainable lineage. Our understanding of who we are and what we are doing is revealed to us at just the right time and in just the right way. Our interconnectedness with our Godliness and with each other is us living as one planet within *the heart* of God. Along my journey of seeking greater consciousness and a burning desire to raise my own, I became acutely aware of the similarities among like-minded paths and people. Moving from a state of wholeness, I began to honor all paths and related to each of them in beautiful ways. Superconsciously, I would seek the Godliness in others, and I would talk to the godliness in others like a best friend.

Sometimes I would practice this mentally if I was listening to someone's sufferings. Other times, I would pray for the things I wanted for myself, for others. It's like gift giving. I always know what to give others. I give them what I would want for myself. It works every time. Spiritual solutions work every time. One day, I was sitting with a friend I had come to respect in the spiritual experience when he shouted out, "Jesus Christ is the savior of the world!"

We chuckled together for a few moments, and then there was dead silence. I had been curious about unknown prejudices I still held that could be negating the sunlight of the Spirit. In my morning meditation, I began to ask the question: "Who am I in Christ consciousness?"

The answers to this question returned magnificent responsiveness during my day, and each time I experienced a collection of numerology synchronicity and the drawing of my attention to symbols that represented light, I felt closer to Christ consciousness that day. I repeatedly asked the question: *Who am I in Christ consciousness?* The embodiment of joy prompted me to continue asking this question day after day as the answers built upon themselves. What was the Jesus Christ piece? Obviously, it wasn't the first time I had heard Jesus Christ referred to as "the savior of the world."

I had even been saved by Jesus Christ in the fifth grade on a Christian retreat. I remembered it being a very sacred ceremony during a lovely weekend, but no further action or information was available to me at that time. I was a guest on the retreat with my friend's family. It was an honor to be invited at the age of nine, but then my family moved—and that was that. I again visited the calling of Jesus Christ at a Christian church in Baton Rouge, Louisiana, called Healing Place Church, while I was studying for my bachelor's degree. I had a marvelous spiritual experience then, but I had no idea how to work with Christ energy. I still held the thought that Christ energy was outside of myself and unreachable. I couldn't relate to how others were so mesmerized by Jesus Christ all the time.

I certainly felt good after church, but I was unconsciously suffering tremendously from buried emotions of childhood trauma. The stories told in church were inspiring, but I didn't know how to rightly relate my life to them in a prospering way. The character defects I had adopted as coping mechanisms kept me locked down in a victim state of existence. The bedevilments were the manifestations of my negative core beliefs. *I am not safe* was at the center of my manifesting nucleus. Being defeated by this serious handicap, it took a lot of effort to continue going to church, especially since access to what was being delivered wasn't given. My self-centeredness was bored and frustrated by this type of schooling. Although inspiring, I didn't get better by hearing a story I couldn't relate to. It just wasn't desirable to me. I needed to hear the story I could relate to and how that story came to be whole. I fell prey to the social acceptance of making my outsides "look good," and that was good enough. I interpreted Jesus Christ as an outside thing, and that is as far as my lower-nature self could perceive. My lower-self mentality, mostly negative ego, made me out to be different: an outsider. I was ashamed of who I was, and what had happened to me, so I lived in a state of merciless survival of the shame and guilt. I never felt authentic at church; rather, I was an image of what I wanted others to see—but I never really showed up for the right reasons.

So there I was twenty years later, after the evolutionary process of the psychic change, when my friend blurts out, out of the blue: "Jesus Christ is the savior of the world!" In amazement, I nearly fell over. Did I just *begin to hear*? His words sung straight to my heart like wind chimes. I could hear it, I could feel it, and as if my heart were the North Star, the Christ consciousness was within me. Was the Christ consciousness within me what I was becoming in atonement? Right doing could only happen with "at-one-ment" with our inner portal to the Master of Light. As I became restored to sanity, *knowing thyself* was evident. Is this what the application of the spiritual principles was revealing to me? That Christ consciousness wasn't an outside thing? That Christ was a state of consciousness totally attainable here in atonement? Wait, is that right? I was having *a coming to Jesus Christ.*

I began testing the waters in meditation by repeating the name as a mantra: "Jesus Christ, Jesus Christ, Jesus Christ." I felt tingling. I felt peace. I felt the presence of love. The access to this new understanding became available in a way that was still unexplainable. I began to remember all the times I stared at Jesus Christ on the wooden cross and thought it was something outside of myself. In this belief, all previous teachings remained unreachable for me. Had I missed the entire boat? Did everyone know that Christ consciousness was *within* us? The theology was incomprehensible, and I hadn't had the access to understand scripture.

The hidden knowledge was being revealed to me, full circle. The hidden *Christ from within* was the great adventure awaiting me. Christ consciousness was the best show on Earth. The love force was the force of Christ consciousness all along, and because it loved me so much, it had waited patiently for my recognition, and my calling it by name. I jumped up! I needed a magic word. *Click, click, click* came to mind as it brought the magic of Dorothy in *The Wizard of Oz* and her magical powers to return home. All it required was just three clicks of the heels of her ruby-red slippers. I would apply the magic now: "Jesus Christ, Jesus Christ, Jesus Christ!" *Click, click, click.* My friend and I joyfully laughed. Our joy filled the entire room. Heavenly bliss was among us. I can't wait to see what good comes from this.

To be continued . . .

EPILOGUE

God is love and God is forgiveness; therefore I AM love and I AM forgiveness.

It all centers on intention. If I AM is aligned with the will of God, then our seeking includes the highest expressions of humility in our actions. When a circumstance or situation appears, these manifestations are opportunities to see who *I AM* and where *I AM* in my willingness to serve God's will. I cannot experience something on the physical plane that I am not responsible for; therefore, I take these intimate encounters from other gods-in-training very seriously. Doing our absolute best to discern our part takes spiritual principle action. Ascension into greater expressions of creation is accessible to all of us by Divine right. Not all humans are aware they are in training to be gods on the physical plane. This creates an even greater opportunity for humility. For through prayers of others, we can speak directly to the God consciousness in others. Certain things we come across that deeply resonate within our souls can be nourished by our connection to one who has all power and all knowledge. God is always presenting the most direct path for me to get out of my own way and be in the grace of life. Wherever I am unwilling to see oneness in others, I will forever remain outside of the Miracle of Life in those areas. In essence, I block myself from the Sunlight of the Spirit in areas of perceived separateness. Denying the I AM within me is an inappropriate use of my will (it is the action of God-less or less of God). I am already forgiven through grace. The master program of life is a time-space continuum where we are spiritual beings in evolution. We are having a human experience for 100 years of that evolution. We are becoming gods. Our acceptance of our God consciousness allows for our spiritual inheritance to flow to us. There are many teachings and opportunities to strengthen our soul structure through the perceived obstacles in our life's journey. They come in many forms as upgrades to our soul structure. The spiritual awakening is what allows us to remember our work on the altruistic plane. Self-reliance is the breakthrough of being freed from the bondage of self. By our walk of inner faith, the illuminated path presents our life contracts in the Great Work. This is the richness we get to take with us beyond the human experience and into the next thing.

ACKNOWLEDGMENTS

To God, M+, the members of Alcoholics Anonymous, the practitioners of yoga, the guides in the Modern Mystery School, and all beings for allowing me this opportunity to share my experiences of strength and hope.

The spiritual principles are infinite in nature. In other words, each time we apply one, our illuminated path is revealed to us. The same principle applied repeatedly can offer both infinite power and knowledge based on where we are in the master program of life. The master program of life is the blueprint for the human. More specifically, our humanoid systems activate within the Earth plane, allowing for our gifts and talents to come to full fruition. This allows us to experience greater portions of creation.

Another word for principle is "law." The principles are laws that possess a spiritual essence within the physical existence. As the currents in the ocean are responsible for our planetary weather, the spiritual principles are part of the earth/human system and are responsible for our sustainable ecosystems. Our internal ecosystems are where we live emotionally, and the humanoid depends on sustainable development. These principles can be discovered through sacred texts, by seeking a greater consciousness, and through an infinite number of ways both known and unknown.

Appropriation of the spiritual principles is our Divine right. As we apply them, our rightly aligned systems produce peaceful solutions that build upon themselves. The feeling of aliveness that occurs between the discovery of a principle and the application of it sets in motion the great adventure of life. The great adventure of life is understanding with absolute certainty that God is within me, and that with this full surrender of who I am at the core level, I open myself up to an outcome I haven't thought of yet. A consistent approach to the connectivity between our inward unseen light and spiritual principles draws us closer to accepting our godliness. Accepting our godliness equates to accepting the responsibility of life. Wherever we are unwilling to accept responsibility is the place where we are currently suffering.

Dynamic flow is the standard for human existence. The flow of light from the One Who Has All Power and All Knowledge into us as we give, receive, and reciprocate with others is our recognition of this flow. The intimacy we yearn for is found within our consciousness with the light and the principles of light. Our duty is to internalize them, and this is where our independence is born.

In this book, there are five spiritual principles presented with corresponding events to assist in understanding each principle. Through retrospect, I relay personal powerlessness and the behaviors responsible for a mindset rooted only in human will. I then move into descriptions of the attitudes and actions that developed from an inner freedom state as a direct result of aligning human will with the will of God. Beyond words, this book begets a spiritual experience unto you all its own. My true part here, then, is to deliver my experiences in this writing—and let the spiritual principles do their thing and speak to you directly.

ABOUT THE AUTHOR

Amielle Zay Marcotte is an American author, spiritual guide, yoga teacher, and higher-consciousness leader. She is the cofounder of LSI Nutraceuticals, a high-vibration health products company. Marcotte is a highly accomplished aviator who has used her global jet-setting position to become more aware of her calling of world service.

Visit the author's website, houseofmarcotte.com, or scan the QR code below to connect on Instagram.

Made in the USA
Monee, IL
07 July 2026

56551658R00092